Williamsburg

by

Lisa Oliver Monroe

Williamsburg (*Tourist Town Guides*®)
© 2010 by Lisa Oliver Monroe

Published by:
Channel Lake, Inc., P.O. Box 1771, New York, NY 10156-1771
http://www.channellake.com

Author: Lisa Oliver Monroe
Cover Design: Julianna Lee
Editorial and Page Layout: Quadrum Solutions (http://www.quadrumltd.com)
Front Cover Photos:
"Pocahontas at Historic Jamestowne" © Lisa Oliver Monroe
"Horse and Carriage" © Lisa Oliver Monroe
"Governor's Palace" © iStockphoto.com/phakimata
Back Cover Photo:
"President's Park" © Lisa Oliver Monroe

Published in April, 2010

ISBN: 978-1-935455-05-9

Disclaimer: The information in this book has been checked for accuracy. However, neither the publisher nor the author may be held liable for errors or omissions. *Use this book at your own risk.* To obtain the latest information, we recommend that you contact the vendors directly. If you do find an error, let us know at corrections@channellake.com

Channel Lake, Inc. is not affiliated with the vendors mentioned in this book, and the vendors have not authorized, approved or endorsed the information contained herein. This book contains the opinions of the author, and your experience may vary.

For more information, visit http://www.touristtown.com

Help Our Environment!

Even when on vacation, your responsibility to protect the environment does not end. Here are some ways you can help our planet without spoiling your fun:

★ Ask your hotel staff not to clean your towels and bed linens each day. This reduces water waste and detergent pollution.

★ Turn off the lights, heater, and/or air conditioner when you leave your hotel room, and keep that thermostat low!

★ Use public transportation when available. Tourist trolleys are very popular, and they are usually cheaper and easier than a car.

★ Recycle everything you can, and properly dispose of rubbish in labeled receptacles.

Tourist towns consume a lot of energy. Have fun, but don't be wasteful. Please do your part to ensure that these attractions are around for future generations to visit and enjoy.

ACKNOWLEDGEMENTS

Dedicated to the memory of my father Garland Woodrow Oliver—a welder by trade—an archaeologist, naturalist and artist at heart.

I would like to acknowledge and thank the following persons for their support, encouragement and patience during the creation of this book, or at other times in my life: my friends Jeannie Pierce, K. Karen Bristow, Tanya Quisenberry and Carolyn Chuck; my sons Mark T. Monroe and Eric K. Monroe; mother Jessie B. Rowe; brother G. Scott Oliver; special family members, Greti K. Monroe and Douglas C. Battram; stepfather Eddie Rowe; my longtime mentor and friend Elsa Cooke Verbyla; and publisher Dirk Vanderwilt.

I also want to thank those persons who were especially helpful during my research for this book: Barbara Brown, Colonial Williamsburg Foundation; Mike Litterst, National Park Service; Bruce Wilson and Chris Smith, Busch Gardens Williamsburg; Bob Harris, Greater Williamsburg Chamber and Tourism Alliance; Tracy Perkins, Jamestown-Yorktown Foundation; and Williamsburg resident Giles B. Cooke.

Many additional thanks to all the kind, helpful and interesting people I encountered in my many travels to Williamsburg, Jamestown and Yorktown.

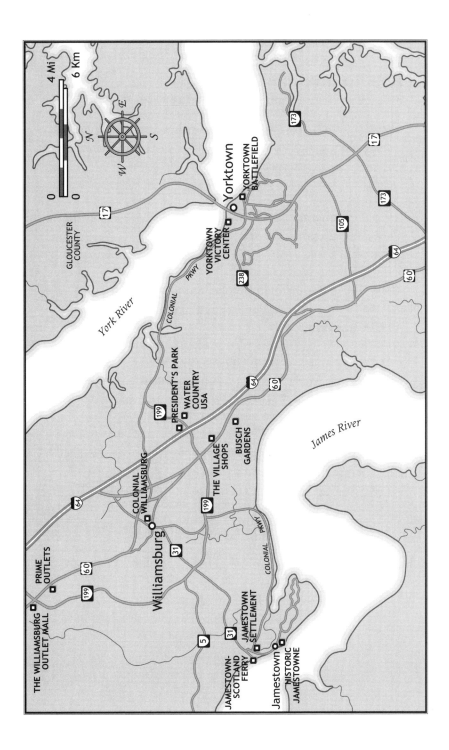

How to Use this Book

✪

Tourist Town Guides® makes it easy to find exactly what you are looking for! Just flip to a chapter or section that interests you. The tabs on the margins will help you find your way quickly.

Attractions are usually listed by subject groups. Attractions may have an address, Web site (🖱), and/or telephone number (☎) listed.

Must-See Attractions: Headlining must-see attractions, or those that are otherwise iconic or defining, are designated with the ✪ **Must See!** symbol.

Coverage: This book is not all-inclusive. It is comprehensive, with many different options for entertainment, dining, shopping, etc. but there are many establishments not listed here.

Prices: At the end of many attraction listings is a general pricing reference, indicated by dollar signs, relative to other attractions in the region. The scale is from "$" (least expensive) to "$$$" (most expensive). Contact the attraction directly for specific pricing information.

Table of Contents

Introduction

The Williamsburg area is a special place to visit because of its unique history and the one-of-a-kind experiences it offers. It gives visitors opportunities to not only learn about history through observation, but also to explore what life was like in the earliest days of America through interactive experiences.

A visit to Williamsburg is, for many visitors, a step back in time. While the area offers many of the modern conveniences of a thriving tourist town, it still evokes an historic sense of place. It preserves part of the American legacy.

I was born in Williamsburg because my hometown of Gloucester across the York River did not have a hospital in the 1960s. Over the years, I've spent many days in Williamsburg. My first Williamsburg memories were shopping sprees to the **Williamsburg Pottery** with my family and elementary school field trips to Colonial Williamsburg and **Jamestown Settlement**. As a teen, it was a thrill to go to the newly opened **Busch Gardens**, and one of my earliest jobs was working as a desk clerk at a motel on Richmond Road.

Having grown up in such an historic area makes one somewhat take it for granted. The research, travels, and experiences involved in creating this travel book have given me a whole new appreciation for the area. It made me realize how fortunate I am to live in an area with such rich history and has inspired me to continue exploring and learning. I've tried as much as possible to weave history and interesting facts I've come across into the travel information in this book to inspire you as well.

The book covers Jamestown, America's first permanent English settlement; Colonial Williamsburg, where colonial heritage is preserved in the country's largest living history museum; and Yorktown, where the country valiantly won her independence from British rule.

In addition to these historical sites, many modern adventures await visitors to the area, from world-class theme parks like Busch Gardens and Water Country USA, to top-rated golf courses like the Golden Horseshoe, and Kingsmill. The area is also one of the best outlet shopping locations in the U.S.

AREA ORIENTATION

Virginia has three peninsulas, which are like fingers stretching from its mainland eastward into rivers. These feed into one of the nation's great tidal estuaries, the Chesapeake Bay. Williamsburg lies on the lower of these three peninsulas nestled between the James and York rivers. It is just northwest of Yorktown, Newport News, and Hampton, in order of proximity. These localities fall lower on the same peninsula. Norfolk is farther south. Williamsburg is located in the commonwealth's Hampton Roads region about midway between Richmond and Norfolk.

One thing worth noting is that Williamsburg is technically an independent city adjacent to James City and York counties. In general, though, James City is casually referred to as Williamsburg, whether talking about the municipal area or not. The county is adjacent to New Kent and Charles City counties to the west, York County, and the City of Newport News to the east. Across the James River to the south is Surry County and across the York to the north is Gloucester County.

Williamsburg is connected to Yorktown and Jamestown by the scenic 23-mile Colonial Parkway in an area referred to as the Historic Triangle. Yorktown is where America's independence was won and Jamestown is the site of the first permanent English settlement and the original capital of Virginia. Williamsburg is within about 15 minutes of either location by car. From the parkway, you can take in beautiful water vistas. Heading to Jamestown, sections of the national parkway overlook the James River, while traveling to Yorktown, much of the parkway runs along the York. The scenery is magnificent in either direction.

The Williamsburg area is part of the mid-Atlantic Coastal Plain, and lies about 86 miles above sea level. It is typically low land dominated by tidal waters and salt marshes. The York and James wind inland to feed smaller rivers and many creeks, which are more muddy than sandy, and some even a bit swampy. The shores and inland areas are dominated by the ever-present loblolly pines, cedars, oaks, dogwoods, and other trees.

HISTORY

Native Americans lived in Virginia about 17,000 years before any Europeans ventured here. The earliest people were hunters and gatherers who lived in small groups, camping along streams within a large set territory.

Between 8,000 and 1,200 B.C., the climate became more habitable as glaciers melted away. The natives continued to move about, but they traveled in larger groups and stayed within smaller areas, as the land became richer.

Over the years, these native people grew very good at living off the land. By 4,000 B.C. they began to make tools like axes to build houses and cut trees for fire. The clearings they made altered the natural environment to their advantage. Berry bushes and saplings grew in the clearings, attracting many animals, which they hunted for food.

These people did not begin settling into villages until between 1,000 and 3,000 years ago. They engaged in early farming, and ate vegetables like squash, gourds and greens. They hunted animals like bear, deer, squirrel and muskrat. In this area, they also fed on fish, crabs, oysters, clams, and turtles which were plentiful here. Their houses gradually grew bigger and the villages more complex.

The Native Americans here were part of the Algonquin Empire which inhabited most of Virginia's coastal plain. They were known as the Powhatan Indians. By the time the Europeans first arrived here, these native people were well organized and flourishing.

EUROPEAN SETTLERS ARRIVE

The first known Europeans to have set foot here were the Spanish in 1570. They reportedly built a mission along the York River, but were killed by natives within months. An English expedition came a decade later, but failed because the group lacked proper supplies.

In the early 1600s, Sir Walter Raleigh and Sir Humphrey Gilbert also attempted to settle in Virginia, but failed. Raleigh transferred his interests to the Virginia Company of London, a group of investors, in 1606.

Sponsored by the company, a group of 104 men led by Captain Christopher Newport arrived in May of 1607 at Jamestown. It was to become the first permanent English settlement in North America. These settlers came 13 years before the Pilgrims landed at Plymouth Rock.

The Jamestown settlers faced many hardships including sickness and lack of food, water, and survival skills. Hostilities also grew between them and the natives as the two groups competed for the same natural resources.

In 1608, Newport sailed back to England, returning to Virginia with more supplies and people, including the first two women. It was in the same year that Captain John Smith was elected president of the governing council. He had been instrumental in developing trade relations with the natives. He was injured not long after his election, however, and had to go back to England, never to return to Jamestown.

Hardships escalated after Smith's departure and the settlers were close to sailing back to England when more supplies and people arrived in 1610. They came under a second charter by the king, calling for a governor to lead Virginia.

Industries like glassmaking and wood production began in the settlement, but none were very profitable, until John Rolfe introduced tobacco as a cash crop. As tobacco farming required large plots of land and labor, the industry helped the colony to grow. The settlers soon expanded out from Jamestown, taking more and more land from the natives.

Given that growing tobacco required plenty of labor, the settlers began using indentured servants. The first Africans were serving in the colony as indentured servants by 1619. They were brought from Ndongo in Angola, where they were captured by the Portuguese. By mid-century, colonists had begun the practice of owning African slaves for life.

The first representative government in British America was established at Jamestown when a general assembly met in 1619. A war with the Powhatan Indians followed in 1622 and two years later, the king dissolved the Virginia Company and established Virginia as a royal colony. Jamestown remained at the center of life in Virginia both politically and socially until 1699.

That same year, colonial leaders successfully petitioned the Virginia Assembly to relocate the capital of Virginia to Middle Plantation, five miles inland of Jamestown. This was partially due to the destruction caused by Bacon's Rebellion. In 1676, Nathaniel Bacon led a group of settlers against Native Americans in defiance of Governor William Berkeley. Berkeley had refused to go after the Indians who'd slain 300-plus colonists along the Potomac River. Bacon drove Berkeley out of Jamestown twice that year and ultimately set fires, which destroyed many of the town's buildings including the church and statehouse.

When it became the capital city, Middle Plantation was renamed Williamsburg in honor of England's reigning King William III.

WILLIAMSBURG: THE NEW CAPITAL OF VIRGINIA

In 1699, Williamsburg became the capital of Virginia, the largest and wealthiest British colony in the New World. That same year, Royal Governor Francis Nicholson ordered the design for the city. It was to include a mile-long main street (Duke of Gloucester Street), with the **College of William and Mary** to the west and the Capitol to the east. The center of the town was to include a market square. The **Governor's Palace** was to lie to the north, symbolizing the king's supremacy.

Williamsburg was the first planned city in America. It was laid out in an orderly grid pattern and its structures were built to certain set standards. There were minimum sizes for houses; setbacks and roofs even had to have a certain degree of pitch.

As more buildings in the city were erected, Williamsburg quickly became the hub of Virginia politics, economics, and religion. The College of William and Mary, which had been completed in 1699 before the rest of the city also made Williamsburg a center for learning. The college was founded in 1693 under a charter granted by its namesakes, King William III and Queen Mary II. It's the second oldest college in the nation, and its Sir Christopher Wren building is the oldest college building in the United States.

The people of the vibrant new city of Williamsburg practiced all sorts of trades and crafts. There were blacksmiths, printers, gunsmiths, wigmakers, bakers, weavers, potters, and more. They also ran shops, taverns, and inns.

The colonial city eventually included a post office, magazine and guardhouse, churches, taverns, shops, homes, offices, and many other buildings.

In this city, the rights of the colonists were eventually debated and the seeds of the American Revolution sown. Therefore, many of the buildings here have specific historical significance. Thomas Jefferson, Patrick Henry, and other patriots were said to have begun plotting the rebellion at the **Raleigh Tavern**. Fierce debates over British taxation were held at the Capitol, where Benedict Arnold later raised the British flag. The magazine or arsenal was the site of the Gunpowder Incident, an event leading many Southern colonies to join the revolution.

The **George Wythe House** served as General Washington's headquarters shortly before the siege at Yorktown.

Williamsburg served as capital of Virginia for 81 years, after which Richmond became the new capital in 1780. Richmond was a more central location as Virginia's population expanded westward. The capital was also moved to protect it from British forces.

During the Civil War's Peninsular Campaign, a battle took place at Williamsburg's Fort Magruder in May of 1862. Union troops advanced north to the area with thoughts of taking Richmond following a Confederate retreat at Yorktown. The Battle of Williamsburg involved over 40,000 Union and 31,000 Confederate soldiers, and resulted in close to 4,000 casualties. The Union army led by Major General George McClellan suffered more than 2,000 casualties and the South led by Major General James Longstreet, suffered around 1,500.

Prior to the battle, Williamsburg had hosted Confederate troops who fortified the area with defensive earthworks. Following the battle, the city existed in a relative state of upheaval and uncertainty as Union soldiers occupied the city intermittently until the close of the war.

RE-CREATING A COLONIAL VILLAGE

The restoration of Colonial Williamsburg became a passion for John D. Rockefeller Jr. from 1926 until his death in 1960. The wealthy philanthropist first learned of the city's historic buildings from Rev. W.A.R. Godwin. The rector of the historic **Bruton Parish Church** in Williamsburg, Godwin saw the value in the old buildings and dreamed of preserving them for posterity.

The two men at first began a small-scale project to preserve a few of the most important buildings. Rockefeller chose the **Sir Christopher Wren Building** at the **College of William and Mary** as the first building to be restored. It is the oldest college building in the United States built from 1695 to 1700.

He then purchased the **Ludwell-Paradise House**, the first building in the exhibit area to be purchased for restoration, even though **Raleigh Tavern** was the first building to actually be exhibited. The restoration project eventually expanded to include 85 percent of the original area. More than 80 original structures were preserved through Rockefeller's generosity. He also funded the reconstruction of many buildings and built new ones like the **Williamsburg Inn** to accommodate visitors.

Colonial Williamsburg today includes 88 original buildings and hundreds of others that were reconstructed on brick foundations left over from the colonial period.

WILLIAMSBURG TODAY

Williamsburg is a small city of close to 13,000 residents adjacent to James City and York counties, but it has more of a hometown feel. It lacks the high-rise buildings, large industrial areas, and traffic woes of larger cities. It is part of Virginia's Hampton Roads region.

Keep in mind that the city of Williamsburg is just a little over nine square miles, and that the adjacent James City County is often casually referred to as Williamsburg. Places like **Busch Gardens Williamsburg, Williamsburg Pottery, Williamsburg Outlet Mall**, and many other places using the word "Williamsburg" in their names are not technically in the city.

Williamsburg is very much a tourist town as well as college town, much busier with tourists during the summer months and with college students the rest of the year. The college enrolls about 7,500 students annually. Not surprisingly, the Colonial Williamsburg Foundation and the **College of William and Mary** are the city's major employers. Over 10,000 workers come to the city to work, while a couple thousand commute to work in neighboring cities like Newport News, Hampton, and Norfolk.

Williamsburg is among the top tourist destinations in Virginia and has the highest per capita annual retail sales of any locality in the state. Colonial Williamsburg sells about three-quarter of a million tickets annually and the larger area hosts between five to eight million visitors each year.

Visitor Information

Close to 40 percent of this area's visitors actually come from other parts of the commonwealth, many taking long weekend getaways. A good portion of visitors also come from other east coast states like the Carolinas, Maryland, Florida, New York, and New Jersey. Texas, Pennsylvania, and Ohio are also among the top ten origin states for Williamsburg tourists. Not surprisingly, over three quarters of the visitors to the area come by automobile.

It's a popular destination for both couples and families. Over 60 percent of visitors here are married and more than 40 percent are traveling with children.

Williamsburg is accessible by air, road, or rail, so tourists can choose the mode of transportation that they find convenient. The easiest way to get around once you're here is by car, with lots of free parking available at most places.

ARRIVING BY AIRPLANE

There are three international airports approximately within an hour's drive of Williamsburg. Due to the distance and travel time, carefully consider either of the two closer airports listed first. Car rentals are available at all three.

The Newport News/Williamsburg International Airport *(airport code: PHF* ☎ *757.877.0221)* is the closest. It is located in the Denbigh area of Newport News, an easy half-hour from Williamsburg by car. The airport has three carriers, but you can still get a direct flight from some cities. These include Boston, New York (La Guardia), Atlanta, Orlando, Philadelphia, and Charlotte.

Visitor Information

Richmond International *(airport code: RIC* ☎ *804.226.3000)* is a little farther away to the west off I-64. It has nine carriers offering direct flights from a few more cities. The drive from here is a little longer, but still easy because the airport's near I-64, which goes straight through Williamsburg.

Norfolk International *(airport code: ORF* ☎ *757.857.3351)* is farther away than the other two, and traffic is often heavier in this area. If you're flying in here, it is better to avoid arriving during morning or afternoon rush hours. Also expect at least an hour's drive to Williamsburg. Despite the extra distance, the ride is worth it for the great water view on the Hampton Roads Bridge-Tunnel. Again, the bridge-tunnel is great unless you're stuck here in a traffic jam.

Williamsburg does have its own general aviation airport for small planes. **The Williamsburg Jamestown Airport** *(airport code: JGG* ☎ *757.229.9256)* includes a pilot shop and restaurant. **Charly's Airport Restaurant** serves surprisingly delicious soups, freshly baked breads, and homemade desserts.

ARRIVING BY CAR

Travelers coming from the east and west can get to Williamsburg via Interstate 64. Those coming from up and down the east coast can get to 64 via Interstates 95 or 295 (the latter detours around the city of Richmond). For a route that's not all highway, visitors from north and south can get off I-95 around Fredericksburg and come via U.S. Rt. 17 South. This will take you through several rural counties and towns and over the York River via the George P. Coleman Memorial Bridge. The bridge has a toll but you only pay it going north. Traveling along this route will provide you with a view of the Yorktown beach and then 13 scenic miles of the Colonial Parkway to Williamsburg. This is a good route if you're coming during the day. At night, the parkway is very dark and might be confusing for motorists not familiar to the area. Plus, drivers have to watch out for deer. There are also many other roads which you can take and which run through the Williamsburg area. These include State Routes 199, 143, and 60.

ARRIVING BY TRAIN

Williamsburg has an **Amtrak station** *(Code: WBG,* 🖱 *amtrak.com)* located at 468 North Boundary Street just minutes from the Historic Area. You can get here from points on Amtrak's Northeast Regional Route via Washington D.C. The route runs through D.C. stretching from Boston to Lynchburg, Virginia. The train ride from D.C. to Williamsburg takes about four hours. You can also get to D.C. via other Amtrak routes and then eventually to Williamsburg.

WHEN TO COME

Summer is the busiest tourist season here, and it's the time when many families visit. It is a great time to come if you want to take full advantage of beaches like Yorktown and water parks like **Water Country USA**. Just expect larger crowds at popular tourist attractions and longer lines at places like **Busch Gardens**.

Traffic in the area is also much heavier in the summer, because interstate highways like I-64 around Williamsburg are used heavily as a thoroughfare for vacationers traveling to Virginia Beach, Nags Head, and other East Coast spots as well as points farther south.

Traffic on interstate highways in the area greatly decreases following Labor Day, which is when public schools resume in Virginia. Crowds also die down at most area tourist spots at this time of year.

Fall is a great time for couples to travel to the area, as things move at a slower pace and there are lesser crowds and shorter lines. It's also easier to view exhibits at the area museums, since not as many people are vying to see the same thing.

Williamsburg has quite a bit to offer now in the winter, especially around the holidays. Colonial Williamsburg is decorated in 18th-century style and holds special programs. Also, Busch Gardens' new **Christmas Town**, which debuted in 2009, opens weekends Thanksgiving through New Year's Eve. It features more than a million lights, a 45-foot Christmas tree, holiday shows, shopping opportunities, and much more. Because of the **Great Wolf Lodge's** indoor water park, it's even possible to have a splash of summer fun in the winter.

WHAT TO BRING AND WEAR

This part of Virginia is still fairly conservative when it comes to clothes. Dress modestly and bring lots of casual, yet comfortable clothes. Definitely pack a good pair of comfortable shoes as many of the tourist spots like Jamestown and the **Yorktown Battlefield** require quite a bit of walking. You may also want to bring some water shoes, or sandals if the beach or water parks are on your itinerary.

As Virginia weather can sometimes be very sporadic, it's best to bring at least a light jacket or blazer on your trip regardless of the time of year. You don't have to drag it around. Just keep one in your car to have ready just in case.

Summers get really hot and humid so it's a good idea to pack some light clothes. You'll also need sunscreen although you can easily buy it anywhere once you are here. If you're going to visit any outdoor areas, it is not a bad idea to wear insect repellant either. There are lots of river and wetland areas here, which means there are also plenty of mosquitoes. Several kinds of ticks live here as well, so it's a good idea to check yourself and your children after spending the day outdoors in the warmer months.

AREA TRANSPORTATION

By far the best way to get around in Williamsburg is by car unless you are going to spend your entire visit in the confines of the Historic Area, where you can pretty much walk to everything. Otherwise, things are pretty spread out and you're going to need a car to get around. Taxis are available, but renting a car is probably a better option, unless you're only going to be staying a day or two. Also, some of the vacation packages which cover the main historical sites include bus service back and forth between these locations. If you're buying one of these packages, it might be possible to get by without a car. Just keep in mind that there's a good chance this will limit your options.

If you'd rather leave the driving to someone else once you arrive, the Historic Triangle Shuttle is a good option. It provides transportation from Colonial Williamsburg to Jamestown and Yorktown. Service runs on the hour and half-hour from 9:00 a.m. to 5:00 p.m. from mid-March to early November.

At both Jamestown and Yorktown, additional free shuttle services are also available. At Yorktown, a free trolley makes stops at the historical sites and other areas of interest. The Jamestown Area Shuttle offers free service between **Historic Jamestowne, the Glasshouse, Jamestown Settlement,** and the **Jamestown Information Station**.

Most hotels, restaurants, and shops here have ample free parking. The only time you will most likely have to pay for parking is when visiting Colonial Williamsburg's Historic Area. Parking there is fairly inexpensive, running around $1 per hour.

WEATHER

The climate and temperatures in Virginia are moderate, although they can both sometimes be unpredictable. This is especially true of the milder climates of fall and spring. Hurricane watches and warnings are likely to occur at least a couple of times a year as well, during the fall or even late summer.

The summers can get really humid and can reach temperatures hovering in the 100° bracket, although the 80s are more typical – the humidity can make it seem closer to 100 though. Even in the hot season, expect a chilly day once in a while.

The winter climate can range from mild to moderate to extremely cold depending on the year. In general, December is fairly mild, and late January and February are the coldest months. March can also sometimes be quite cold, with a late snowfall now and then.

Colonial Williamsburg

Colonial Williamsburg refers to the Historic Area, plus the Visitor Center, a number of modern lodging and dining facilities, even a spa and golf course. Colonial Williamsburg is run by the Colonial Williamsburg Foundation. It's actually the largest living history museum in the country and also well known as the primary source of knowledge on colonial life in America. It continues to make new discoveries as it researches colonial America and updates its Historic Area and exhibits.

The Historic Area is in essence the living history portion of Colonial Williamsburg, complete with colonial taverns, shops, and other buildings, some restored and some reconstructed. This large area is closed to vehicular traffic and extends along Duke of Gloucester Street, which was the main street through the original colonial city. Historic buildings can be found along both sides of the street which extends to the colonial Capitol. The Historic Area extends to the north to Nicholson and North England streets, and along Palace Green leading to the **Governor's Palace**.

Visitors can stroll through the Historic Area and also browse the shops at no charge, but many of the buildings like the Capitol, Governor's Palace, and exhibits demonstrating colonial trades are open only to ticket holders.

Adjacent to the Historic Area are nearby places of interest like the **College of William and Mary** and shops in Merchant's Square and on nearby streets. The square is a modern shopping area with upscale shops and restaurants in a location where a colonial market would have once existed. The square is owned by the Colonial Williamsburg Foundation, but most of the shops themselves are privately owned.

The Visitor Center is a short distance away, as are modern lodgings and restaurants operated by the foundation. It's the best place to begin your Colonial Williamsburg visit. There's a lot of free parking and a shuttle bus can take you to the other areas from here. Informative guides can also give you maps and answer any questions you may have.

Places within the Historic Area have been separated into this chapter for those wishing to experience a full colonial experience by dining, shopping, or spending the night in a colonial environment. We've included a separate chapter on the more modern aspects of Colonial Williamsburg such as its world-class spa, golf course, and modern restaurants and lodgings. A third chapter outlines things to do, restaurants, shops, and places to stay within a short walking distance of the Historic Area. These are not part of Colonial Williamsburg.

Consider staying in Colonial Williamsburg lodging because guests can purchase reduced Hotel Guest Passes which provide unlimited daytime access to sites and museums in the Historic Area. They get a 25 percent discount on evening programs.

There are a number of admission options for Colonial Williamsburg. Admission gets visitors into the buildings and exhibits in the Historic Area which require tickets. Prices range from $36 to $58 for adults, but the lower-priced one-day ticket excludes the **Governor's Palace**. Prices for children from 6–17 years run about half the price of adult admission. Children 5 and under get in free.

Consider the American Historic Triangle ticket if you're going to spend several days in the area and want to take in all the historical sites. This ticket gets you unlimited admission for five days to Colonial Williamsburg, **Historic Jamestowne, Jamestown Settlement, Yorktown Battlefield**, and the **Yorktown Victory Center**.

The Historic Area is open 9:00 a.m. to 5:00 p.m. 365 days a year, though hours may vary slightly by season. Evening programs and special events are often held outside regular hours as well.

HISTORIC AREA OVERVIEW

The Colonial Williamsburg Historic Area includes 88 original restored buildings from the 18th and early 19th centuries spread over 301 acres. There are also several hundred reconstructed buildings, most on their original foundations. Most buildings have an exterior identification plate which identifies them by name and as "restored" or "reconstructed," both of which stand for two different things. Restored buildings were intact buildings which were preserved in their original state in the 20th century through efforts by John D. Rockefeller Jr. In contrast, reconstructed buildings were totally recreated based on knowledge and research of the original structures. Most were rebuilt on their original brick foundations which still remained. Visitors may be surprised as they explore the Historic Area to find that not all buildings here are open or on exhibit.

The area provides a perfect opportunity to soak up the colonial experience to the degree of your choice. You can simply stroll along the main route, Duke of Gloucester Street, which runs through the middle of the colonial village and browse through colonial shops. At some point, you are likely to see and hear the Fifes and Drums marching past and you may also witness recreated historical dramas played out in the streets or taverns as part of the Revolutionary City program. You can dine in colonial-style taverns, sampling foods similar to those enjoyed by diners in the 18th century.

To view demonstrations of colonial trades and crafts and to tour many of the buildings in the Historic Area, an admission pass with several options available is required. The basic pass includes most exhibits and buildings for one day, but does not cover the **Governor's Palace**, guided walking tours, behind-the-scenes programs, and other special events. Upgraded and multi-day passes are a good idea for those planning to spend more than a day in this area to really absorb all the colonial experiences available.

A place to begin your visit here is the ticketing booth near Merchant's Square to pick up a weekly program and map. Daily and evening programs change all the time and vary from day to day. Since admission here is not inexpensive, it's a good idea to stroll through the town with your map in advance of purchasing a ticket. Familiarize yourself with the area and denote on your map the areas that you want to explore in more detail. Then purchase the type of admission that will best match the things you want to do and length of time you want to spend during your visit.

Reasonably priced parking is offered near Merchant's Square in both a nice multi-level parking garage and in outdoor lots, and very short term parking is available for free. The indoor garage is a good option and costs about $1 an hour.

COLONIAL THINGS TO SEE AND DO

At Colonial Williamsburg's Historic Area, visitors can actively or passively experience colonial life to the degree they choose. Simply stroll the area and take in a few programs. Or for a total colonial experience, rent a period costume and eat popular colonial fare in an historic tavern setting, converse with costumed "patriots" in dramatic programs which bring history to life, and spend the night in colonial-styled housing. Some of the highlights of the Historic Area have been enumerated below, but this is just a sampling of what the area has to offer and is by no means to be considered an inclusive list.

AFRICAN AMERICAN RELIGION EXHIBIT

(220C Nassau St.) This exhibit explores the religious roots of African-Americans, covering the first slaves and their descendants to the formation of the first black church congregation in Williamsburg. The exhibit is located the Taliaferro-Cole

First Baptist

house donated

the exhibit is

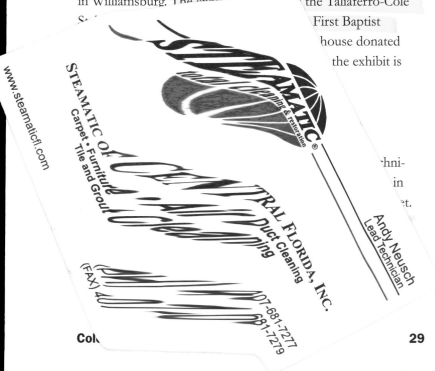

hni-

in

et.

The Bruton Parish churchyard dates to the 17th century and is also open for self-guided tours. A downloadable map with information on the cemetery is available in advance online at the church's Web site.

This Episcopalian parish was first established in 1633 and remains an active church today. The present church building dates to the early 1700s. The parish's first church is believed to have been built in the 1630s, but the location has not been discovered. Later in 1683, a small brick church was completed just north and west of the present church. It was only 60 feet by 24 feet, and after the college was completed and the capital moved to Williamsburg, it was quickly outgrown by its congregation.

The present church building was completed in 1715. It is shaped like a cruciform and is 75 feet long and 28 feet wide with 14.5-foot wings. Additions were later made to the building to make it grander, including the addition of galleries, an enlarged chancel, the Jamestown baptismal font, the Tarpley bell, and a new steeple.

Its churchyard is the final resting place for many influential colonial people from royal governors to local leaders. These include the two children of Martha Custis – who would later marry George Washington – and John Blair, a signer of the U.S. Constitution. Many Confederate soldiers were also interred here during the Civil War when the church served as a makeshift hospital.

The church building is open to visitors from 10:00 a.m. to 4:00 p.m. Mondays through Saturdays, and 12:30 p.m. to 4:30 p.m. on Sundays. However, the church is sometimes closed to tours during the hours allocated for church services, weddings, or funerals. Visitors are invited to join in public worship services if they wish. Church members serve as volunteer guides on the tours.

COLONIAL CAPITOL

(East Duke of Gloucester St.) Knowledgeable guides will take you on a short tour of the main areas of this reconstructed Capitol, including the **House of Burgesses** and the **General Court**. The tour takes about 30 minutes as the guide relates the significance of events that took place in the colonial era to our lives today. The five large portraits visitors will see hanging in the House of Burgesses are high-quality reproductions of the original royal portraits painted in the 1700s. There are also evening programs here which highlight the political events that occurred here.

This is the site where Patrick Henry made his Caesar-Brutus speech against the Stamp Act of 1765 and was sworn in as Governor of Virginia in 1776. George Washington, George Mason, George Wythe, Thomas Jefferson, and others also participated in spirited legislative debates here leading to the Revolution.

The reconstructed Capitol celebrated its 75th anniversary in 2009. It was built on the unearthed original foundation to match the original capitol building constructed in 1705. That first capitol burnt in 1747 and was replaced by a second one. This building was used as the Capitol until the end of 1779. It was later used to house an admiralty court and several schools. It was destroyed in 1832 while it was vacant.

Since more details existed regarding the specifications of the original capitol, the reconstructed building was based on that building rather than the second.

The current reconstructed building was completed and dedicated in 1934 with a meeting of the Virginia General Assembly. Since that time, this legislative body holds special joint commemorative sessions here in Williamsburg. Also, a naturalization ceremony is held here annually to welcome a new group of American citizens, a process in the Capitol dating to 300 years ago. Admission to the Capitol is included in most Colonial Williamsburg tickets.

GEORGE WYTHE HOUSE

(101 Palace Green St.) This restored Georgian-style home was built in 1755. The two-story brick residence has been restored and furnished to appear as it may have looked when George and Elizabeth Wythe lived in it during the late 18th century. Wythe was a lawyer, Virginia's first signer of the Declaration of Independence and mentor to Thomas Jefferson and John Marshall. Thomas Jefferson stayed in the home with his family in 1776 and General George Washington used it as his headquarters before the siege of Yorktown. French General Rochambeau later used it following the war. Admission to the home is included in most Colonial Williamsburg tickets.

GOVERNOR'S PALACE

(300 Palace Green St.) This reconstructed palace celebrated its 75th anniversary in 2009. The original was considered one of the finest buildings in British North America. It was home to two Virginia royal governors, five lieutenant royal governors, and Virginia's first two governors, Patrick Henry and Thomas Jefferson. Today's palace is furnished to show how it would have looked when it was the residence of the Earl of Dunmore, Virginia's last royal governor. Visitors can tour the palace where they can see the ballroom, bedrooms, dining room, pantry, and other rooms. In the palace's kitchen, the Historic Foodways program presents cooking demonstrations in the preparation of foods using 18th-century methods. Visitors can tour the elaborate palace gardens and mazes outdoors. Admission to the palace requires the minimum of a Plus Pass.

HISTORIC TRADES

Colonial Williamsburg has more than 70 artisans who practice colonial trades and crafts at 21 sites in the Historic Area. These trades include blacksmithing, cabinet making, masonry, printing and bookbinding, shoemaking, weaving, wig-making, tailoring, and more. Trade shops showing the artisans at work require museum admission. Inside the Weave Room, for example, you might see several weavers spinning wool or dying handmade yarn. Artisans here are not only full-time professional craftspeople, but are interpreters as well and very educated in their trades. They are usually very willing to share information, engage in conversation, and answer questions you may have. Their works, created using colonial methods and of colonial standards, are used throughout the Historic Area.

LUDWELL-PARADISE HOUSE

(207 East Duke of Gloucester St., Historic Area) This home dates to 1755. It is closed to the public, but is significant because it was the first building purchased for restoration by John D. Rockefeller Jr. in 1926. The home was residence of

Lucy Ludwell Paradise in the 1800s. She was the daughter of the home's original owner Philip Ludwell II. The home was also rented during colonial times. The *Virginia Gazette*, a Williamsburg newspaper still in operation today, was once printed here by William Rind and his wife Clementia.

MAGAZINE AND GUARDHOUSE

(103 East Duke of Gloucester St.) Colonial Williamsburg ticket holders can see a collection of original and reproduction cannons and muskets at the Magazine. There are also leather workers and artisan soldiers at work, creating leather, wood, fabric, and metal items. Depending on the season, visitors might get to see a musket as it is fired. They can also join in militia drills. The Gunpowder Incident of April 1775 which ignited the Revolution in Virginia occurred here.

RICHARD CHARLTON'S COFFEEHOUSE

(426 East Duke of Gloucester St.) Tour this reconstructed 18th-century style coffeehouse, the only one in the United States, in small groups. Tours include educational information on the history of the establishment as well as a sampling of colonial treats and beverages like coffee and tea. The building is furnished with reproduction furniture, ceramics, glassware, hardware, maps, prints, advertisements, and other items used in daily colonial life. Depending on the time of visiting the Historic Area, visitors could catch a colonial dramatization or musical performance on the coffeehouse porch. The coffeehouse is the newest of the reconstructed exhibit buildings in the Historic Area that was opened to the public in November 2009. More than ten years of research and planning went into the building. It was constructed on the foundation of the original coffeehouse, which was converted from a storehouse prior to 1765. Prominent Williamsburg residents, including colonial businessmen and government officials congregated here for informal meetings to discuss politics or the latest gossip. They would have sipped China tea imported from England, coffee, and other hot beverages, as well as wine, beer, and liquor. Foods like fish, shellfish, meat, and game would have been served.

TAVERN GHOST WALKS

(☎ 800.HISTORY/800.447.8679) A Colonial Williamsburg guide will tell stories of ghosts that inhabit the buildings as you walk through the colonial town. The tour is all outside. Those taking the tour receive a collector souvenir pin. Cost is a little more than $10 for adults and a little less for children under 12.

PLAY BOOTH THEATER

(210 Palace Green St.) Colonial Williamsburg ticket holders can catch a scene from a popular 18th-century play at this open-air theater. Makeshift theaters became popular on public days in Williamsburg during colonial times. Performances vary and usually last about 30 minutes. They are held as the weather permits.

MUSEUMS IN THE HISTORIC AREA

The term "museum" here can be a bit confusing, as Colonial Williamsburg's Historic Area is basically one large living history museum in itself. However, in this section, the buildings within the Historic Area which function as modern museum facilities have been included. Two of the museums are located in the Public Hospital on West Francis Street, which is itself a museum. It houses the **Abby Aldrich Rockefeller Folk Art Museum** and the **DeWitt Wallace Decorative Arts Museum**. There is also a small café serving sandwiches, wraps, soups, beverages, and other light foods. A small but wonderful gift shop sells reproduction and handcrafted art, books, craft items, and jewelry among other things.

Bassett Hall, the fourth museum, is located a short distance away on the same street which is open to vehicular traffic. Therefore, it's possible to park close to all the museums when traveling by car.

Museum admission is included in most Colonial Williamsburg tickets. Visitors can purchase a separate museums-only ticket for admittance to the museums listed below for around $10 or $5 for youth 6-17. As it can take the good portion of a day to explore them, the less expensive museums-only ticket might be a good option for anyone with limited time to spend in Colonial Williamsburg or for those primarily interested in the museum exhibits.

ABBY ALDRICH ROCKEFELLER FOLK ART MUSEUM
(326 West Francis St. ☎ 757.220.7984

☗ colonialwilliamsburg.org/history/museums) This museum has a great collection of folk art. It features pieces created by colonial to contemporary artists, using a large variety of materials at hand, from metal and wood to leather and cloth. Exhibits on display include furniture, toys, needlework, sculpture, paintings, wood carvings, and more. There's a lovely exhibit of handmade quilts of assorted patterns. There is also a room of folk music instruments with audio buttons. Visitors will find many unusual items like a sculpture made of ice cream scoops and the

Hippocerous, a phonograph machine shaped like a hippopotamus. Admission to the museum is included in most Colonial Williamsburg tickets, or visitors may purchase a museums-only ticket for around $10. The museum is open daily.

BASSETT HALL
(522 East Francis St. ☎ 757.220.7453
☗ colonialwilliamsburg.org/history/museums) This 18th-century home was the former residence of John D. Rockefeller Jr. and his wife Abby Aldrich Rockefeller. It was reopened to the public in 2002 following a two-year renovation. Visitors should allow about an hour here. This includes time to view the exhibits, a 12-minute introductory film, and to take part in a 30-minute guided tour of the home and explore outbuildings. The museum's exhibits integrate the lives of the Rockefellers with the early years of Williamsburg's restoration, which was funded by Rockefeller. Admission to the home is included in most Colonial Williamsburg tickets, or visitors may purchase a museums-only ticket for around $10. Bassett Hall stays open daily.

DEWITT WALLACE DECORATIVE ARTS MUSEUM
(326 West Francis St. ☎ 757.220.7984
☗ colonialwilliamsburg.org/history/museums) This museum is housed in the Public Hospital along with the **Abby Aldrich Rockefeller Folk Art Museum**. The **Elizabeth Ridgely** and **Miodrag Blagojevich Gallery** located here has a large collection of American furniture dating from the colonial period through the 19th century. Pieces are from three main areas of the country: Eastern Virginia, New England, and Pennsylvania. Many woods and woodworking techniques are represented

in the pieces, which range from desks and chairs to large armoires. There are some unusual carved pieces like a *Masonic Master's Armchair* dating from 1765. The museum's ongoing exhibits include displays of military and civilian firearms, colonial coins and currency, pottery, ceramics, metals, and more. The museum has ongoing plus many special exhibits. A recent exhibit featured antique toys like dolls, intricately decorated dollhouses, and model trains of metal and wood, with some items borrowed from the neighboring folk art museum. Admission to the museum, which is open daily, is included in most Colonial Williamsburg tickets, or visitors may purchase a museums-only ticket for around $10.

PUBLIC HOSPITAL

(326 West Francis St. ☎ 757.220.7984

☻ **history.org/Almanack/places/hb/hbhos.cfm)** This reconstructed building represents the first mental hospital in the United States built in the early 1770s. It has six exhibits in a small exhibit hallway. Several show the living conditions of patients and how these evolved from the 18th to the 19th centuries. Other exhibits show the restraints used, as well as instruments like needles and early machines used to treat the hospital's patients. There are also portraits of some of the key persons associated with the hospital, like William Galt. He was mayor of Williamsburg during the late 18th century. As mayor he had the responsibility of running the Public Hospital. Besides the hospital exhibits, this large building houses both the **Abby Aldrich Rockefeller Folk Art** and the **DeWitt Wallace Decorative Arts** museums. Admission to the building is included in most Colonial Williamsburg tickets, or visitors may purchase a museums-only ticket for around $10. Visitors are welcome on any day as the museums stays open daily.

RESTAURANTS IN THE HISTORIC AREA

The taverns of Colonial Williamsburg provide visitors with a chance to dine in buildings constructed and decorated in colonial fashion. Many also offer the foods that colonial residents would have eaten, prepared with the same ingredients and cooking methods.

Diners are served by a knowledgeable staff dressed in colonial garb. They can provide information about colonial foods and dining habits if you have any questions. Many of the taverns also hold varying programs which allow diners to interact with interpreters portraying famous colonial personalities or to listen to music performed on period instruments.

Each tavern's days and hours of operation vary by season so call for reservations if you'd like to dine in a specific tavern. While some of the taverns require reservations, others welcome walk-ins. Parking for tavern dining is offered at designated areas at no charge.

The scale for the dinner entrées is as follows: under $10 = ($), $10-$20 = ($$), and above $20 = ($$$).

CHOWNING'S TAVERN
(109 E. Duke of Gloucester St. ☎ 757.229.2141
🖱 colonialwilliamsburgresort.com/dining/chownings) This tavern (pronounced chew-nings) specializes in traditional pit barbecue. It is the most casual of the historic taverns and caters to families. It serves beef brisket, pulled pork barbecue, turkey legs, and grilled chicken sandwiches for lunch. An outdoor stand in the tavern garden also sells quick foods like sandwiches, soups, stews, and salads to go. In the

early evenings, an entertainment program called "Gambols" is offered with music, magic, and colonial games suitable for the entire family. Costumed balladeers lead diners in games and sing-alongs. Guests can snack on peanuts and other light dinner foods. Beverages include wines and ales, plus ginger ale and draft root beer. After 8:00 p.m., the program caters to adult audiences. No reservations needed. *($)*

CHRISTIANA CAMPBELL'S TAVERN

(101 South Waller St. ☎ 757.229.2141

🖳 colonialwilliamsburgresort.com/dining/christianacampbells) The original tavern was George Washington's favorite because of its hospitality and delicious seafood. Today's tavern serves lots of seafood entrées including its signature lump crab cakes served with sweet potato muffins, spoon bread, and Mrs. Campbell's cabbage slaw. A children's menu includes macaroni and cheese, hamburgers, and more served with applesauce on the side. A couple days each week, the tavern hosts an 18th-century style tea with Mrs. Campbell. Reservations are required. *($$$)*

KING'S ARMS TAVERN

(416 East Duke of Gloucester St. ☎ 757.229.2141

🖳 colonialwilliamsburgresort.com/dining/kingsarms) Dine in this colonial-styled tavern based on the original King's Arms Tavern where Virginia's gentry and most influential leaders once feasted. Try colonial delicacies à la carte, or get the fixed-price sampler. This includes the tavern's trademark peanut soup, a boneless breast of chicken with ham, a side of potatoes, mushrooms and tarragon sauce, and homemade bread.

The sampler includes your choice of rice pudding or pecan pie for dessert. The tavern also offers a hot breakfast buffet with "Citizens of the Revolution" seasonally on select days of the week. During this program, guests can engage in conversation with their favorite colonial patriots while they dine. The tavern stays open for lunch and dinner, with reservations recommended for dinner. Children's menus are available. *($$$)*

RALEIGH TAVERN BAKERY

(410 E. Duke of Gloucester St. ☎ 757.229.2141
colonialwilliamsburgresort.com/dining/raleigh-tavern-bakery)
This bakery is located behind **Raleigh Tavern**. It serves delicious baked items like gingerbread, cakes and cookies, soups, ham biscuits, and hot and cold beverages. No reservations are necessary for a meal here. *($)*

SHIELDS TAVERN

(422 East Duke of Gloucester St. ☎ 757.229.2141
colonialwilliamsburgresort.com/dining/shieldstavern) The original Shields Tavern catered to the lesser gentry and upper middle-class locals and travelers. Today's tavern serves seafood like seafood gumbo and buttermilk fried oysters, pot roast, buffalo meatloaf, pulled pork barbecue, and other sandwiches and wraps. Diners can also try colonial favorites like Bubble and Squeak or Welsh Rarebit. A full bar serves beers, ales, and specialty drinks with a colonial flair like apple cider rum and spiced wine. Open for lunch and dinner, the tavern does not require reservations. *($$$)*

COLONIAL-STYLE SHOPPING

Shopping in this area is like taking a trip back in history. The shops sell items that would have been sold in colonial stores, many crafted on-site by Colonial Williamsburg artisans, plus some modern gifts and souvenirs. They are run by costumed interpreters who are usually very knowledgeable about the items they sell and colonial history in general. They are a great source of information if you have questions about the buildings, items for sale, or colonial history.

The shops listed here are some of those located within the pedestrian-only Historic Area and run by the Colonial Williamsburg Foundation, with one exception. The **Bruton Parish Shop** is a private shop run by **Bruton Parish Church** and not part of Colonial Williamsburg, though it is located in the Historic Area.

BRUTON PARISH SHOP

(331 West Duke of Gloucester St.) This shop adjoins the Parish House of **Bruton Parish Church** and is located near the church. It is divided into two areas. One area offers inspirational and religious items, but also many other gift items including namesake souvenirs. Shoppers can buy everything from plush animals and toys to beautiful dishes and figurines. The other area is for seasonal items and is converted into a lovely Christmas parlor from the fall through the holidays. It sells Goebel nativities, a large selection of ornaments and cards, and other holiday items. In the rear of the seasonal shop, there is a door leading to a small chapel, which is open to visitors for quiet prayer and contemplation. The shop is open daily. Proceeds benefit the church's outreach ministry.

THE GOLDEN BALL

(406 East Duke of Gloucester St.) This shop sells sterling silver jewelry created by the Colonial Williamsburg silversmith. It also sells reproduction jewelry in 14-karat gold, gemstone rings, pendants, charms, and more.

JOHN GREENHOW STORE

(106 West Duke of Gloucester St.) This reconstructed shop sells food items like fruit preserves, bread and cake mixes, wooden utensils, coffee in souvenir bags, and crocks among other things.

MARKET SQUARE

(103 East Duke of Gloucester St.) Shoppers can purchase hats, pottery, souvenirs, and toys at this outdoor booth. Colonial costumes for children can also be rented here.

MARY DICKINSON STORE

(107 West Duke of Gloucester St.) This shop sells ladies' colonial clothing like petticoats, caps and mittens, plus a nice selection of hats. Jewelry, scented soaps, and other toiletries are also sold here. The store is open daily.

POST OFFICE

(304 East Duke of Gloucester St.) This reconstructed building has a book area and also sells writing tablets, slate boards and chalks, inkwells, quill pens, maps, reproduction prints, and more. Copies of the *Virginia Gazette* newspaper from the colonial times are printed downstairs each morning by Colonial Williamsburg artisans. It stays open daily.

PRENTIS STORE

(214 East Duke of Gloucester St.) This restored shop sells pottery, leather goods, iron hardware, furniture, and baskets made by Colonial Williamsburg tradespersons.

TARPLEY'S STORE

(401 East Duke of Gloucester St.) This is a fun shop. It is housed in a reconstructed building which mirrors the colonial store once run by Tarpley, Thompson & Company. According to the original store's handbill, it sold cloth like Venetian poplins and Manchester velvets, china, looking glasses, silver ware, bread baskets, bearskins, and much more. Today's store sells all kinds of candies and candied fruit by the quarter pound plus wrapped chocolate bars. Shoppers will also find colonial books, dolls, toys, soaps, crocks, and hats. In addition, there's a nice selection of old-fashioned musical instruments like tin whistles, maple fifes, and melody harps.

COLONIAL HOUSING – HISTORIC LODGING

(136 E. Francis St. ☎ 757.253.2277/1.800.HISTORY
🖱 colonialwilliamsburgresort.com/hotels/deluxe/colonialhouses)
For an authentic colonial experience, you can stay in one of 26 colonial-style buildings. These are complete with period furnishings and many have fireplaces and canopy beds. Some of the buildings are as small as one room and others have rooms that can be combined to accommodate up the 32 guests. Some accommodations are handicapped-accessible, but not all.

The buildings are not all houses. They are instead reconstructed or restored taverns, kitchens, offices, and even shop buildings scattered throughout the Historic Area. Each is named and has its own unique history. **Market Square Tavern**, for example, is a restored building once frequented by Thomas Jefferson while he was studying law under George Wythe. The building has six guest rooms, each with private baths. There is an original fireplace in the great room on the first floor.

Cary Grant stayed at **The Quarter**, another restored building open to guests, while filming *The Howards of Virginia* in 1942. It is a small building, probably used to house indentured servants during colonial times.

Nicholas-Tyler Office and Laundry is another lodging choice. The property was once owned by President John Tyler while he was running for office in 1840. The building is reconstructed.

Lodgers here have full access to the indoor/outdoor pools and fitness center at the **Spa of Colonial Williamsburg**. No pets or smoking allowed. *($$)*

Colonial Williamsburg

In 1699, Williamsburg became the capital of Virginia, the largest and wealthiest British colony in the New World.

MODERN COLONIAL WILLIAMSBURG

Besides the Historic Area, Colonial Williamsburg offers wonderful modern shops, dining experiences, a world-class golf course, luxurious spa, and an assortment of lodging options to suit various budgets.

THINGS TO SEE AND DO

If you have had your fill of history and crave a taste of modernity, Colonial Williamsburg offers visitors world-class lodgings and golf courses, an upscale luxury spa and modern fitness facilities. Whether you're looking for a place to stay where you will be pampered and served like royalty or a place that caters to family fun, there are lodging and dining options to suit just about anyone's taste and budget, plus lots of places to shop.

VISITOR CENTER

The Williamsburg Visitor Center is a great place to begin your visit to Colonial Williamsburg. It's easy to get to and there's a large free parking area. There are booths for purchasing tickets, and helpful guides who can give tips to help you enjoy your visit, provide maps and directions of the area, and answer questions. This large, open building has informational displays, several shops, and two theaters which show an historical film called *Williamsburg: The Story of a Patriot*.

Williamsburg Booksellers features a large selection of regional and historical books on topics like ghosts and legends, the Civil and Revolutionary wars, and Colonial Williamsburg. There's also a selection of historical fiction. **A Learning**

Resource Center has educational resources for teachers, parents, and students. The bookstore has a small coffee bar with an outdoor patio. It offers espresso drinks, brewed coffees and teas, cold drinks, and snack items.

On the other side of the building, Williamsburg Revolutions sells gifts, home décor, and souvenirs. The store has a large selection of costumed dolls. They represent men, women, and children in various colonial roles, from soldier to musician. Some of the other items sold here include fruit presses, crocks, shirts, soaps, stationery, and goose quill pens.

From the Visitor Center, take a shuttle bus to the other Colonial Williamsburg attractions. This is the best way to get a feel for the layout of the area before deciding where to start exploring.

KIMBALL THEATRE

(Merchant's Square ☎ 757.565.8588 ● kimballtheatre.com) This small theater located in Merchant's Square offers films as well as live performances by musical and theater groups from the community, the College of William and Mary, and beyond. Daily schedules are posted outside the theater, but are also available online where tickets can be purchased in advance. The theater has a rich history dating to the 1930s. It was one of John D. Rockefeller's favorite places to visit. Walt Disney also frequented the theater when visiting Williamsburg. Its box office opens daily around 4:00 p.m.

GOLDEN HORSESHOE GOLF CLUB

401 South England St. ☎ 757.220.7696/800.648.6653 for toll-free golf reservations ● colonialwilliamsburgresort.com) This award-winning Colonial Williamsburg club features three

separate golf courses in beautiful surroundings secluded from residential and commercial hustle and bustle.

The club's two 18-hole courses each have their own club-houses, restaurants, and golf shops. The Gold Course is located just off the grounds of the **Williamsburg Inn** and the **Spa of Colonial Williamsburg** for those who want the luxuries of a resort. The Green Course is a little farther away.

The Gold Course is a traditional par-71 course designed by Robert Trent Jones Sr. and renovated by his son Rees Jones in 1999. The 6,817-yard course first opened in 1963 and the professional course record was set four years later by Jack Nicklaus. The course has a USGA slope rating of 144.

The course has received many honors. It was named as one of "America's 100 Greatest Public Courses" in 2009 and several previous years. It was also recognized by *Golf Magazine* in its "Top 100 Courses You Can Play." Its 16th hole was lauded by the magazine as one of the "Top 500 Golf Holes in the World."

The more contemporary Green Course opened in 1991 was designed by the elder and younger Jones' team. It's a 7,120-yard, par-72 course with a USGA slope rating of 138.

The Spotswood Course is a nine-hole course popular with tourists as a warm-up course and also for golfing with the family. The par-31 course has one par 5 hole, two par 4s, and six par 3s.

The Golden Horseshoe has hosted a number of championship events. These include the NCAA Division I Men's Championship in 2007, the U.S. Women's Amateur Public

Links Championship in 2004, and the U.S. Kids Golf World Championship 2002–2005.

Green fees range from $79 to $165 based on the season. The club also offers four levels of membership for those interested in regular golf outings here.

MERCHANT'S SQUARE

This upscale shopping area is adjacent to Colonial Williamsburg's Historic Area. It consists of an open brick walkway with seating surrounded by more than 40 shops and restaurants. Many are unique, one-of-a-kind businesses, while there are also a few chains like Williams-Sonoma and Baskin-Robbins. The **Kimball Theatre** is also located in the square.

Merchant's Square is owned by Colonial Williamsburg, though most of the shops are privately owned. The exceptions are **Williamsburg at Home, Williamsburg Celebrations**, and **Williamsburg Craft House**, which are Colonial Williamsburg shops selling Williamsburg-brand items. These are all open daily.

Williamsburg at Home is a large store displaying and selling fine home furnishings. These include furniture, bedding, rugs, linens, fabrics, light fixtures, and wall hangings. **Williamsburg Craft House** offers jewelry, ceramic items, folk art, glassware, and dinnerware. It sells many personalized gifts and offers engraving as well. **Williamsburg Celebrations** is a store that carries seasonal items including floral arrangements, holiday decorations, collectibles, and garden accessories.

During the warmer months from May through October, the **Williamsburg Farmers Market** is open at Merchant's Square on Saturdays. This market offers fresh local produce, berries, jams, herbs, cut flowers, decorative gourds, wreaths, and handmade soaps sold by approximately 30 vendors. Special markets are also held the Saturdays before and after Thanksgiving and on the second Saturday in December. These offer a variety of foods and gifts fit for the season.

THE SPA OF COLONIAL WILLIAMSBURG
(307 South England St. ☎ 757.220.7720

🖰 colonialwilliamsburgresort.com) This modern 20,000-square-foot spa offers a variety of treatments and massages for individuals and couples. Treatments range from an Indian-inspired, hot stones spa to a colonial herbal spa experience. There are treatments with various purposes including rejuvenating or exfoliating the skin.

Massages range from sports to Shea butter massages. There's even a Wi-Fi massage to target areas most stressed by use of modern electronic devices. A sampler massage combines aromatherapy, sports, Swedish, reflexology, and hot stones techniques.

Couples can have side-by-side treatments in the Rose Garden Suite with a deluxe soaking tub, private shower, restroom, and a large treatment room.

Other services offered at the spa include an assortment of body scrubs and wraps, bath experiences, plus skin care, and nail care. There's a hair salon and a fitness center as well. The spa sells Naturopathica and TRUE Cosmetics products.

MODERN PLACES TO STAY

Colonial Williamsburg's lodging options range from the economical **Governor's Inn**, perfect for those on a budget to the **Woodland Hotel and Suites**, ideal for families because of its children's day camp and recreation activities, to the luxurious world-class **Williamsburg Inn**, which has been the accommodation of choice of U.S. presidents and royalty.

Standard room rate in peak season starts at under $100 = ($), $100-$200 = ($$), and above $200 = ($$$).

GOVERNOR'S INN

(506 N. Henry St. ☎ 757.253.2277/1.800.HISTORY
⬤ colonialwilliamsburgresort.com/hotels/value/governorsinn)
This mid-sized hotel is the most affordable of Colonial Williamsburg's lodgings. It's the best value for families watching their pocket books and is within a five-minute walk of the Historic Area. There's a very large outdoor pool and guests are provided a complimentary continental breakfast. They can also use recreational facilities at the nearby **Woodlands Hotels and Suites**. No pets or smoking allowed. *($)*

WILLIAMSBURG INN

(136 E. Francis St. ☎ 757.253.2277/1.800.HISTORY
⬤ colonialwilliamsburgresort.com/hotels/premium/
williamsburginn) Colonial Williamsburg considers this hotel the "crown jewel" of its lodgings and the choice for its most discriminating guests. It has accommodated royalty, U.S. presidents, heads of state, actors, television personalities, and many other luminaries. This list includes the likes of Sir Winston

Churchill, General Dwight D. Eisenhower, President and Mrs. George H.W. Bush, Emperor Hirohito of Japan, Shirley Temple, Christopher Plummer, Lady Margaret Thatcher, Jane Pauley, Tom Selleck, Gary Trudeau, and Matt Lauer. Queen Elizabeth II and Prince Philip stayed here during the queen's first visit to America in 1957 and again in 2007, when she took part in Jamestown's 400th anniversary celebration.

The hotel opened in 1937 and underwent an extensive renovation in 2001 to enhance its guests' experiences while keeping authenticity in mind. Everything, from period wallpapers to floor finishes and furniture arrangements were replicated. Handmade silk window treatments were even handcrafted in Colonial Williamsburg to replace the ones which had hung at the inn.

Today's guests are treated with amenities literally fit for a queen. Rooms feature king or queen beds with fine linens, night spreads, and an evening turndown tray. They have views of courtyards, the golf course, lawn bowling, gardens, and the Historic Area. Some rooms have canopy beds with separate sitting and working areas. Spacious bathrooms have twin marble vanities, Italian marble-enclosed soaking tubs, and large marble showers. Baths feature hair dryers, lighted magnifying mirrors, and plush terrycloth bathrobes.

The inn has three dining areas. The **Regency Room** has crystal chandeliers, palm-leafed columns, and leather upholstered furniture. Windows all around the room provide lovely views of the grounds. The restaurant serves classic American cuisine with a European flair. Some of the house specialties are crabmeat Randolph, grilled gulf shrimp, Chateaubriand, and for dessert, hazelnut ice cream cake with marinated strawberries and Kahlua fudge sauce.

The **Terrace Room** hosts a seasonal afternoon tea with custom-blended teas, scones, finger sandwiches, pastries, champagne, and sparkling cider. It is also open in the evening for cocktails, hors d'oeuvres, and other light foods. The adjacent **Restoration Bar** is a popular spot for evening cocktails and socializing.

The Williamsburg Inn opened in 1937 in response to the need for lodgings by visitors of the newly opened but popular Historic Area. It was built under close supervision and with strong attention to detail by John D. Rockefeller Jr. He wanted the inn to exude the comfort of a gracious country estate rather than that of a hotel. That was partially because his many personal friends and acquaintances frequently visited the area.

Rockefeller worked with architect William Perry to design and decorate the inn in the Regency style of 19th-century England. A sample guest room was even built at the Rockefeller Center in New York City to help them visualize décor. Close attention was paid to the comfort of guests and the hotel was the first in the country to have central air conditioning.

Guests here can avail of the **Golden Horseshoe Golf Club**, the **Spa of Colonial Williamsburg**, a fitness center, indoor pool, and much more. Recreational activities include tennis, lawn bowling, biking, and croquet. No pets or smoking allowed. *($$$)*

THE WILLIAMSBURG LODGE

(310 South England St. ☎ 757.253.2277/1.800.HISTORY ⬮ colonialwilliamsburgresort.com/hotels/premium/ williamsburglodge) This fine resort hotel was recently renovated, expanded, and decorated with art mimicking pieces and patterns seen at the **Abby Aldrich Rockefeller Folk Art Museum** in the Historic Area. The lodge has more than 300 rooms and is Colonial Williamsburg's primary conference hotel, catering to large groups and hosting special events. It has a very large conference center with two ballrooms, banquet space, and close to 30 meeting rooms.

There's a 190-seat restaurant which serves Southern-style dishes with a contemporary flair. Meals are prepared under the direction of Executive Chef Rhys Lewis, who also oversees the complex's large lounge area and bar. Guests can stay at the lodge or one of several large new guest houses. Rooms and suites are comfortable and homey. They have the look and feel of bedrooms in a fine Southern home. *($$$)*

THE WOODLANDS HOTEL AND SUITES

(105 Visitor Center Dr. ☎ 757.253.2277/1.800.HISTORY ⬮ colonialwilliamsburgresort.com/hotels/deluxe/woodlands) This contemporary three-story hotel has 300 rooms and is located next to the **Visitor Center**. It is great for families or couples. Its Colonial Kids Club provides an educational day-camp experience for children between 5–12 years in the mornings or afternoons in the summer. This can allow parents the chance to have a break or explore the area together as a couple. The camp engages children in a variety of supervised activities like colonial games, arts and crafts, and visits to sites in the Historic Area.

The hotel also has recreational activities suitable for the entire family like mini-golf, walking trails, horseshoes, and ping pong. There's also a huge outdoor pool, fitness center, and gift shop.

Rooms and suites are both available here. Rooms feature cable television, complimentary wireless Internet access, desks, and a lounge chair that converts to a sofa bed. Suites include separate sitting rooms and a convenience counter with microwave, small refrigerator, and sink. A large, popular restaurant called **HUZZAH!** is adjacent to the hotel. It is casual and family-friendly, serving burgers, wraps, hand-tossed pizza, homemade soups, salads and desserts, in addition to items on its children's menu. *($$)*

Williamsburg Near The Historic Area

There are many wonderful shops and restaurants in Merchant's Square and on nearby Prince George Street, as well as the **College of William and Mary**. Places listed in this section are within walking distance of the Historic Area, but are not run by the Colonial Williamsburg Foundation.

THE COLLEGE OF WILLIAM AND MARY

(Admissions Office: 116 Jamestown Rd. ☎ Main: 757.221.4000 🖱 wm.edu) Since the College of William and Mary is a public institution, its grounds are open to the public. It's a nice place for a stroll if the weather permits. There are also several buildings on campus that are worth touring. These include the Sir Christopher Wren Building, the Muscarelle Museum of Art, and the Earl Gregg Swem Library.

Besides the buildings that are open for tour and the art museum, there is also a self-guided walking Plant Tour of Woody Species which begins at the Wren building. To follow the set-tour sequence, visitors must download a map online ahead of time. The "Enjoying the Great Outdoors" chapter provides details about the tour.

The **Campus Shop**, located at 425 Prince George St., is the best place to go to buy William and Mary souvenirs and apparel.

The College of William and Mary is the second oldest college in the United States. Harvard is the oldest, but it is said that William and Mary was actually in the works earlier than Harvard, with plans stalled due to an uprising of Native Americans.

The charter for the college was granted on February 8, 1693, by King William III and Queen Mary II of England. It was the first college in North America to receive a royal charter. Work was begun on the college's first building, the Sir Christopher Wren Building, in 1695. Today, it holds the distinction of being the country's oldest college building.

The college is sometimes called the "Alma Mater of a Nation" due to its ties to the founding fathers. Three presidents received their undergraduate degrees from William and Mary, including Thomas Jefferson, John Tyler, and James Monroe. George Washington also received his surveyor's license from the college and later became its first chancellor.

Besides the three presidents, it is alma mater to four former Supreme Court justices, numerous congressman and senators, diplomats, businesspersons, and military leaders. Just a few notable personalities of today who graduated William and Mary include the *Daily Show's* Jon Stewart, actress Glenn Close, and NFL coach Sean McDermott.

THE SIR CHRISTOPHER WREN BUILDING

(111 Jamestown Rd.) at the College of William and Mary is the oldest restored building in Williamsburg. It is also the oldest college building in the United States. Construction on the building began in 1695 before Williamsburg was named the capital of Virginia. It was originally called the College Building, and it was completed in 1700. It was later renamed after Sir Christopher Wren, who is credited with the building's design.

This was the main college building housing classrooms, a dining hall, library and faculty room. It also served as residence for the president of the college. The basement housed the servants' quarters and a kitchen.

The building was gutted by fire five years later and two more times in 1859 and 1862. It was set ablaze by Union soldiers the last time. The interior of the structure was rebuilt each time.

This was the first building chosen by John D. Rockefeller Jr. to be restored as part of the Colonial Williamsburg restoration he funded. It also underwent another major restoration and repair project in 1999–2000.

Today the Wren continues to be used for academics, housing faculty offices and classrooms. It also houses an Information Center with displays on the building's history. There are student proctors and docents available to provide additional information and answer visitors' questions. The Grammar School Room in the Wren shows the way a colonial classroom looked. The building is open 10:00 a.m. to 5:00 p.m. weekdays, and 9:00 a.m. to 5:00 p.m. weekends.

THE EARL GREGG SWEM LIBRARY

(400 Landrum Rd.) has a Special Collections Research Center, which houses a permanent exhibit on Chief Justice Warren E. Burger. The exhibit of Burger's recreated office consists of many objects belonging to him. These range from a leather briefcase to the bench chair he used while serving on the Supreme Court. Burger was chancellor of the College of William and Mary from 1986 to 1993. The college is home to his papers, donated by his son Wade in 1996.

MUSCARELLE MUSEUM OF ART

(Lamberson Hall, 611 Jamestown Rd. ☎ 757.221.2711
🖱 wm.edu/muscarelle) This small art museum is located on the
William and Mary campus off Jamestown Road right next to
Phi Beta Kappa Hall. This museum is known to run special
exhibits on famous artists, like Andy Warhol. It also has a
permanent collection of over 4,000 items, although not all are
displayed. Divided into several galleries, the museum houses
special exhibits upstairs, in the Cheek, Graves, and North
Galleries. Paintings and sculptures on display on the main floor
galleries represent American and international artists. One
of the most well-known paintings at the museum is Georgia
O'Keeffe's *White Flower*. Some of the other artists represented
include Titian, Hung Liu, James Rosenquist, Diego Velazquez,
William Hamilton, John Singleton Copley, and Preston
Dickinson. A print gallery downstairs features works on paper.
The museum is open daily except Mondays and most national
holidays. Regular admission is $5 and special exhibits cost an
additional charge. You can park at the museum for free, but
after parking, a pass from the museum needs to be acquired to
stick on the car so that your vehicle is not ticketed.

ACCOMMODATIONS NEAR COLONIAL WILLIAMSBURG

Besides Colonial Williamsburg lodging, there are a few places to
stay within walking distance of the Historic Area.

Standard room rate in peak season starts at under $100 = ($),
$100-$200 = ($$), and above $200 = ($$$).

CLARION HOTEL HISTORIC DISTRICT

(351 York St. ☎ 757.229.4100 🖱 clarionhotel.com/ hotel-williamsburg-virginia-VA622?promo=gglocal) This hotel is only a couple minutes from Colonial Williamsburg. Its amenities include a heated indoor pool, hot tub, exercise room, game room, and a public computer with Internet access. Rooms feature free high-speed wireless Internet access, hair dryers, desks, cable/satellite television, and irons and ironing boards. There are also some rooms available with kitchens. There is a restaurant and cocktail lounge called Bourbon Street, where guests can have a meal or relax in the evening. This hotel is non-smoking, supports green practices, and is pet-friendly. *($)*

THE FIFE & DRUM INN

(441 Prince George St. ☎ 757.345.1776 🖱 fifeanddruminn.com) This quaint inn is located on Prince George Street adjacent to Merchant's Square and the **College of William and Mary**, and is perfect for anyone spending more than one day in the Historic Area. It is actually the city's smallest hotel because of the amenities it offers. These include private baths and phone lines, cable television, Wi-Fi, hair dryers, and bathrobes. The inn features seven rooms, plus two suites, and the Drummers Cottage. This adorable brick cottage features its own little white picket fence and mini flagpole with an American flag. It is located nearby and sleeps up to six. Each room is themed and decorated with 19th-century folk art, interesting artifacts, and memorabilia. In one room, you'll find a signed letter from John D. Rockefeller Jr. and in another, antique postcards from Jamestown's 1907 exposition. Baths include showers with seats. The inn's rustic Common Room has a fireplace and can accommodate 20 diners. A daily breakfast buffet is complimentary. *($$)*

NEWPORT HOUSE BED & BREAKFAST

(710 South Henry St. ☎ 757.229.1775 🖰 newporthousebb.com)
This bed and breakfast is a very unique place for those wanting
to immerse themselves in the colonial experience. It's located
about five minutes from the Historic Area on Henry Street. Built
in 1988 based on designs by colonial architect Peter Harrison,
the bed and breakfast is completely furnished with period
antiques and reproductions. Rooms have four-poster canopy
beds and private bathrooms with showers. Guests are treated to
a full complimentary breakfast prepared with historical colonial
recipes, fresh produce from the home's garden, and usually an
historical seminar. Owners and hosts John and Cathy Millar have
also purchased a nice selection of colonial costumes which their
guests may rent. Also available is an extensive selection of videos
relating to the 18th century. The Millars host colonial dancing in
their home Tuesday evenings, with guests welcomed to join in.
No pets or smoking is allowed. *($$)*

BLUEGREEN PATRICK HENRY INN/PATRICK HENRY SQUARE

(249 York St. ☎ 757.229.9540 🖰 patrickhenryinn.com) The
Patrick Henry Inn is a couple minutes away from Colonial
Williamsburg by car, but not so far away that you couldn't walk.
It is also less than a ten-minute ride to **Busch Gardens**. The
inn may not be luxurious, but is a good value for those on a
budget looking for a fairly inexpensive place to stay near the
Historic Area. It has all the typical amenities plus a small conti-
nental breakfast each morning. There is an outdoor heated
pool and game room. The adjacent Bluegreen Patrick Henry
Square resort has villas with kitchenettes, a fitness center, and

kid's club. No smoking allowed in rooms. Patrick Henry Inn *($)*, Patrick Henry Square *($$)*.

RESTAURANTS NEAR COLONIAL WILLIAMSBURG

There are many wonderful eateries in the area adjacent to Colonial Williamsburg's Historic Area. These range from unassuming diners popular with William and Mary students to fine dining establishments and everything in between. We've included some of the restaurants in Merchant's Square and on nearby Prince George Street because they're within an easy walk of the Historic Area. Restaurants outside of this immediate area are included elsewhere in this book.

The scale for the dinner entrées is as follows: under $10 = ($), $10-$20 = ($$), and above $20 = ($$$).

AROMAS COFFEEHOUSE CAFÉ & BAKESHOP
(431 Prince George St. ☎ 757.221.6676 🖥 aromasworld.com)
This very casual rustic café sells delicious sandwiches, wraps, soups, and salads for lunch and dinner that can be eaten indoors or on the streetside patio. They also offer additional dinner plates like pan-seared scallops or stone-ground grits and shrimp. Breakfast includes traditional items, omelets, French toast, grits, and egg scrambles. Diners can get the latter stuffed with various meats ranging from chorizo sausage to crab, country ham and cheese. They serve all types of beverages from hot teas and espresso drinks to fruit smoothies, beer, and wine. The bakery has a nice selection of gourmet cookies, pastries, and other treats. In the evenings, diners can try two fondues, brie cheese, or chocolate. Children's items are available on the menu. The café is open daily. *($)*

BERRET'S RESTAURANT AND TAPHOUSE GRILLE

(199 South Boundary St. ☎ 757.253.1847

☗ berrets.com) Located in Merchant's Square adjacent to Colonial Williamsburg's Historic Area, this restaurant is a local favorite. The seafood restaurant offers a fine dining experience, while the Taphouse Grille is for more casual dining in the outdoor patio area and closes during colder months. The restaurant features fresh local and regional seafood in season. Dinner entrées are simple yet delicious. Try the very large shrimp stuffed with creamy crabmeat wrapped in prosciutto with tomato fennel sauce or a rib eye steak with onion rings, red bliss potatoes, and sour cherry barbecue sauce. There is an extensive wine list, a full bar with a selection of local microbrews on tap, and a children's menu. *($$$)*

BLUE TALON BISTRO

(420 Prince George St. ☎ 757.476.2583 ☗ bluetalonbistro.com)
This bistro-style restaurant is located on Prince George Street adjacent to Merchant's Square. It has a modern ambience, yet is decorated in rich deep colors that give it a warm feel. It has numerous windows and several dining areas, as well as an outdoor patio. Diners will find an interesting and somewhat eclectic selection of foods here. Order everything from salted cod to chicken and mushroom crêpes for lunch. Dinner entrées range from grilled swordfish to a version of macaroni and cheese served with country ham to game pot pie. This dish is made with rabbit, venison, oxtail, and duck in a red wine sauce, a large assortment of vegetables, and garlic and herbs. Many entrées are served with a delicious lightly seasoned mixed green salad. Open daily for breakfast, lunch, and dinner. The house water is served in chilled glass bottles, a great concept, but it still tastes like chemically-enhanced city water so consider investing in a drink. *($$$)*

A CHEF'S KITCHEN

(501 Prince George St. ☎ 757.564.8500 🖰 achefskitchen.biz)
This restaurant has transformed cooking lessons into a fine culinary experience. Diners watch from tables set in rows, as Chef John Gonzales prepares a gourmet five-course dinner. While doing so he entertains the audience, educates students about the various foods used, and demonstrates how the meals are prepared. The dinners begin with hors d' oeuvres and champagne, and also include three glasses of paired wine and recipes. Dinner cooking classes run around $75 per person. Traditional cooking classes are also available. Class participants get the recipes and can sample prepared dishes, but are not served full meals as in the dinner classes. Traditional classes are about half the price of the dinner classes. Wine pairing classes are also offered. Classes range from two-and-a-half to three hours. Reservations are required and a credit card is needed to hold the reservation. *($$$)*

FAT CANARY

(410 W. Duke of Gloucester St. ☎ 757.229.3333
🖰 **fatcanarywilliamsburg.com)** This upscale restaurant features innovative dishes and a fine selection of wines. Its menu is fairly small, but the food is far from ordinary. Try the pan-seared Monkfish with lemon and fennel risotto, clams, tomato, and chorizo. Or for something a little heartier, how about grilled rack of lamb with mint and pine nut cous cous, ratatouille, and grilled onions? The menu varies seasonally and specials are changed daily. Open nightly for dinner. Reservations are recommended. *($$$)*

LENNY'S GOURMET

(445 Prince George St. ☎ 757.253.0458) This deli-style diner boasts the best sandwiches in town and has a cozy, casual basement-level dining area. It offers a good selection of sandwiches, panini, and wraps at very reasonable prices. Diners can also choose from several salads, sushi rolls, and hot Asian foods like Japanese dumplings or curry rice. The restaurant remains open daily for lunch and dinner. *($)*

RETRO'S GOOD EATS

(435 Prince George St. ☎ 757.253.8816 ✆ retrosgoodeats.com)
Located near the **Fife and Drum Inn**, this is a great place to eat if you like a good hot dog. They sell various types of wieners, including turkey and veggie dogs. Diners can top their dogs with an assortment of toppings ranging from blue cheese slaw, to barbecue, to sweet potato mustard. They also serve burgers, chicken and barbecue sandwiches, soups, and chili. To quench your thirst, they serve limeades, floats, milkshakes, and draft beer. Choose from several flavors of custard for dessert. Retro's Good Eats is open daily. *($)*

THE TRELLIS CAFÉ, RESTAURANT, AND GRILL

(403 East Duke of Gloucester St. ☎ 757.229.8610
✆ thetrellis.com) This restaurant has a great reputation in the area for its food and desserts. It serves lunch and dinner daily in an upscale yet unpretentious setting. Dinner courses have a Southern flair and consist of exquisite combinations. The restaurant is open daily except on Thanksgiving, Christmas, and New Year's. *($$$)*

SHOPS NEAR COLONIAL WILLIAMSBURG

These shops are located in or adjacent to Merchant's Square or right on the edge of the Historic Area. The shops in this up-scale area are generally unique and interesting. They sell many quality items, some handcrafted or one-of-a-kind. Keep in mind though, that with a few exceptions, this is not the ideal place for bargain shopping.

BINNS OF WILLIAMSBURG

(435 West Duke of Gloucester St. ☎ 757.229.3391

☗ **binnsonline.com)** This upscale, two-story clothing store is located in Merchant's Square. It specializes in women's apparel, shoes, jewelry, and cosmetics. They sell top brands like Faberge, Stuart Weitzman, Escada, and St. John. There's a gift boutique here with home décor, crystal, porcelain, and seasonal items. The store sometimes holds special events like lectures and fashion shows and stays open daily.

CAMPUS SHOP

(425 Prince George St. ☎ 757.229.4301

☗ **williamsburgsouvenirco.com)** Shoppers will find lots of apparel and souvenirs for the **College of William and Mary** at this small shop. Take home a "Tribe" hat, tee-shirts, mugs, and more. The shop is located near Merchant's Square and is open daily.

CLOSET ENVY

(409 W. Duke of Gloucester St. ☎ 757.220.0456

☗ **shopclosetenvy.com)** This is an upscale ladies' clothing boutique in Merchant's Square offering personalized service. They sell top brands like Diane Von Furstenberg, Theory, Kooba, and Joe's Jeans. A White + Warren cashmere sweater here will set you back about $180. Open daily except Easter, Thanksgiving, Christmas, and New Year's day.

GALLERY ON MERCHANTS SQUARE ✪ Must See!

(440A Duke of Gloucester St. ☎ 757.564.1787

☗ **galleryonmsq.com)** This large second-story gallery has wonderful open rooms for shoppers and art lovers to browse.

These spacious areas are decorated with a fine mix of original art and antique items ranging from porcelain figurines to large pieces of furniture. Many area artists are represented, as are regional subjects, but the gallery displays works from artists all over America and the world. There are a lot of pieces with maritime and nautical themes, plus an interesting collection of paintings with country scenes, landscapes, flowers, animals, and people. Besides paintings and prints, there's a wonderful collection of sculptures, plus some jewelry and mixed media pieces. The gallery is open daily.

I MUST SAY

(423 Prince George St. ☎ 757.229.2755) This eclectic shop sells silver jewelry and paintings by local artists, plus other handmade jewelry, stationery items, books, furniture, and a nice selection of antique pieces. The antiques are mixed throughout the shop amongst the new items serving as décor. The shop has a selection of gifts for horse and dog lovers. It also sells neat little books to help writers, artists, and book lovers stay organized. The shop is open Mondays through Saturdays.

J. FENTON GALLERY

(110 South Henry St. ☎ 757.221.8200

☋ quiltsunlimited.com/stores/williamsburg/) This wonderful shop sells lots of unique handcrafted items specializing in the work of American artisans. Shoppers will find a large selection of glass items ranging from vases to lamps and even colorful mouth-blown glass balloons. Handcrafted wooden items range from carved walking sticks to sleek polished trinket boxes. This shop also has a large selection of jewelry made by U.S. artists, as well as a wonderful collection of fine kaleidoscopes and Judaic items. You'll find lovely purses, wallets, wall hangings, pottery pieces, and many one-of-a-kind items here. The gallery is open for visits everyday.

JOE'S SOUVENIR

(501 Prince George St. Suite 101 ☎ 757.220.9860) This small shop near Merchant's Square sells some of the most reasonably priced souvenirs in the area. They have a large selection of tee-shirts, hats, key chains, mugs, and children's items, and are open all seven days of the week.

MRS. BONES BOWTIQUE

(110 South Henry St. ☎ 877.767.1308 ☖ mrsbones.com) Located in the Henry Street Shops, this upscale shop caters to those who really want to pamper their pets. Shoppers can find lots of items for indulging their feline and canine friends ranging from gourmet treats to knitted apparel and a large assortment of Mrs. Bones' unique handmade pet collars and leashes. The shop also sells home décor, clothing, art, and other items featuring various breeds of dogs. This shop for the pooches is open daily.

QUEENS COURT LTD.

(439 Prince George St. ☎ 757.565.3649) This store sells some very pretty jewelry, and at very reasonable prices in comparison with some of the other shops near the Historic Area. Open 365 days a year.

THE PEANUT SHOP OF WILLIAMSBURG

(414 Prince George St. ☎ 757.229.3908 ☖ thepeanutshop.com) You can buy Virginia peanuts in almost any flavor imaginable in this shop which has nuts set out in various areas for tasting. They sell spicy and sweet varieties available in all kinds of packaging, from tins to large bags. The shop also sells specialty nuts, Paula Dean sauces and foods, specialty dog treats, gift baskets, and a whole lot more. The shop is open daily.

THE TOYMAKER OF WILLIAMSBURG

(415 W. Duke of Gloucester St. ☎ 757.229.5660
⬤ toymakerofwilliamsburg.com) The Toymaker of Williamsburg is a fun place to browse or buy gifts and toys. It sells everything from modern dolls to colonial tri-corn hats, and classic toys liked tin wind-ups and wooden mazes. The shop also has a very large selection of toy soldiers, figurines, and other toys that let children use their imaginations. You can even purchase educational toys like puzzles, science kits, and craft kits. For a very special gift to give someone, check out the beautiful wooden rocking horses and Radio Flyer wagons. Open daily except Thanksgiving and Christmas days.

WILLIAM AND MARY BOOKSTORE

(345 Duke of Gloucester St. ☎ 757.253.4900
⬤ wm.edu/bookstore/index.php) This large bookstore is located right on the edge of Colonial Williamsburg's Historic Area across the street from Merchant's Square. It is operated by Barnes & Noble, and is in many ways typical of that bookstore chain's regular stores. However, in addition to the mainstream books one might expect to find, the store also sells new and used college textbooks, school and dorm supplies, and William and Mary apparel and souvenirs. The store has a small coffee shop upstairs. The bookstore is open daily.

Busch Gardens Williamsburg

Busch Gardens is a European-themed amusement park known for its entertaining shows and thrilling rides. Griffon, its newest coaster, is the world's tallest and first floorless dive coaster. The park is also well recognized for its beauty and environmental practices. The park was purchased in 2009 by Blackstone, but continues to be operated by Sea World Parks and Entertainment.

It was named the world's most beautiful theme park for the 19th consecutive year in 2009 by the National Amusement Park Historical Association. That's not surprising, as lovely gardens adorn the park around every turn and beside every walkway. The plants seen are grown right here in behind-the-scenes greenhouses and cold frames.

The park is open for its regular season from late March until the end of October. Summer is undoubtedly the best time to go to the park if you are going primarily for the rides, as many offer the opportunity to get wet. Summer is also the busiest time at the park though, which translates into longer lines and waits.

If you're going to the park for the shops, shows, dining and quieter activities, consider going in the spring or fall when you can have a more leisurely visit and there are smaller crowds. Another way to get around the crowds is to purchase a Quick Queue Pass. It allows guests to skip to the front of the line on select rides and attractions, and at times may provide reserved seating for some shows.

The park offers special seasonal events like Howl-O-Scream in the fall. The whole park is transformed to be fun in a scary sort of way, with live ghouls and goblins roaming about after dark. Several rides are shut down for the season and converted to haunted houses, like the Caverns of Darkness.

For the first time in 2009, the park reopened after its regular season for **Christmas Town**. The new attraction runs from Friday through Sunday evenings from Thanksgiving until New Year's Eve. The park is decorated for Christmas Town with more than a million lights and a 45-foot animated Christmas tree. There are special shows, shopping opportunities, and attractions, all holiday-themed. Admission is about a third of the price of regular-season admission.

Regular admission to the park for one day is a little over $60 for adults and just over $50 for children aged 3 to 9. Children 2 years old and younger get in free.

It may be advisable to consider a multiple-day pass for those tourists visiting the park for the first time or for those who will be spending more than a few days in Williamsburg. The park is very large and it is a great deal to experience in one day. This is especially true for visitors interested in seeing the shows and shops as well as trying the rides. Guests can also purchase combined passes which admit them to **Water Country USA** and Busch Gardens.

The park offers a number of multiple-day and combined ticketing options. The 2-Park Discovery Ticket is a good option for those interested in trying both parks. For around $80, guests get unlimited admission to Busch Gardens and Water Country USA for seven consecutive days from the date of first use. The ticket is only good through early fall though. Check for the exact date of expiration.

Virginia residents get a special deal. They can purchase a one-day fun card for around $60. The card can then be used for unlimited visits to the park through early September.

For those serving in the military, Busch Gardens "Here's to Heroes" program offers a single day's free admission for him or her, and up to three direct dependents. Just register online or in the entrance plaza of the park. You must show your Department of Defense photo identification.

Those watching their budgets can get a number of deals by going to the Busch Gardens Web site before going to the park. For example, guests can purchase and print an online parking ticket for around $10, saving a couple dollars off the price of paying to park at the gate. There are also various online meal vouchers which allow guests to get meals at a set price. The gold certificate, for example, includes an entrée, two side items or desserts, and a non-alcoholic beverage for around $15. Or buy a snack voucher online for around $3, and redeem it for an ice cream, popcorn, or cotton candy in the park.

Another great way to stretch the vacation dollar is to eat outside the park, especially for those visiting multiple days. You can get your hand stamped at the gate upon leaving, allowing you to return to the park the same day. Pack lunch in a cooler and eat outside the gates. There are also fast-food restaurants like McDonald's, Wendy's, and a combo KFC and Taco Bell restaurant only minutes away on Route 60.

Commemorating your visit to Busch Gardens is easy. There are several areas throughout the park where guests can have individual or family portraits and caricatures made. In France, there is also a photography studio where the whole family can have a photo taken dressed in antique costumes.

For those who want to visit the park, but want to leave the planning and details to someone else, Busch Gardens offers customized vacation packages in combination with other Williamsburg attractions and places of lodging.

PARK AREAS

The 350-acre park is divided into six "countries." These include England, Scotland, Ireland, France, Germany, and Italy. Each country has its own special charm, restaurants, shops, rides and other activities.

ENGLAND

Guests are greeted by the sounds of whimsical flutes as they enter the park through the English village, complete with replicas of Big Ben and the Globe Theatre. Here the whole family can watch a 4-D movie featuring popular Sesame Street characters. Those with a sweet tooth might want to check out **M. Sweet's Confectionary**, with its delicious fudge, chocolate-dipped apples and pretzels, and candies.

From England, guests can proceed on foot to Scotland or they can take the Aeronaut Skyride to France or Germany. These cable coaches are a great way to get an aerial view of the park's rides and attractions. Their use is also recommended to save on walking as the park is huge. They can be a lifesaver at the end of the day when you are ready to leave, but find yourself at the opposite end of the park from the exit.

SCOTLAND

The next country along the pathway is Scotland, where guests can see Clydesdale horses inside the Highland Stables or grazing outside in the fenced pasture. Then up ahead, is a wilder sight of the Loch Ness Monster. This was the original coaster at Busch Gardens when it opened in 1975 and is still one of its most popular rides.

From Scotland, guests can proceed to Germany or Ireland by foot. They can also take a train from the **Tweedside Train Station** to Italy or France. Another fantastic way to save energy, especially later in the day, and it is a lot of fun to boot!

GERMANY

In Germany, guests looking for more leisurely activities can take a slow boat ride on the "Rhine River." Little ones can enter their own mythical play world at **Land of the Dragons** where everything is just their size. They can also try a number of kiddie rides like the junior bumper cars. The whole family can ride the restored antique carousel or embark on a thrilling 3-D adventure, **Curse of DarKastle**.

Thrill seekers can become inverted not once, but six times, on the wild coaster **Alpengeist**. And a trip to Busch Gardens is not really complete without having experienced Oktoberfest while eating a mile-high sandwich at **Das Festhaus**. The shops in Germany are also well worth a browse or two if you have time. The outdoor carnival-style games are loads of fun if you have some extra money and feel lucky. People actually do win if the large prizes being carried around are any indication!

FRANCE

France has two distinct areas. The first is a traditional French village and the other is a rustic French-Canadian trader's village. In the first area, guests can try the world's tallest and first floorless dive coaster, **Griffon**. Its first drop sends riders plunging a 90-degree drop at more than 70 miles per hour. The trader's village is a great place to buy personalized items or have an antique portrait made. Shop here for items ranging from a coonskin hat to a designer leather handbag. Guests can also decorate a pot in **Caribou Pottery** or dine on smoked ribs at the **Trappers Smokehouse**. If the weather is warm, a ride on **Le Scoot Log Flume** is the ultimate-in-fun way to cool off.

ITALY

Italy has a lot of mid-sized rides which are great for all ages. These range from spinning tea cups to the **Roman Rapids**. Just be prepared to get very wet as you drift down the rapids under waterfalls and sprays. Da Vinci's cradle is a great one to try. Little ones can pretend like they are flying in rides like the **Li'l Gliders**. Big "kids" can try **Apollo's Chariot**, a thrilling hyper coaster that drops guests 210 feet in its initial drop. Hopping on a train at the train station in Italy is a great way to get back to Scotland near the park's entrance at closing time.

IRELAND

Last but not least is Ireland, where guests can try a brew in **Grogan's Pub** or sample Irish stew at **Grogan's Grill**. The whimsical shops here are amazing, full of magic and dragons, dolls and play animals. They are likely to delight old and young alike. There are also more practical items like fine wool hats and sweaters made in Ireland. **Europe in the Air** is a high-tech simulated ride the whole family can try. Guests can also visit **Jack Hanna's Wildlife Reserve** to get a glimpse of American bald eagles and grey wolves. There are also a couple of wacky animal shows and an aviary sure to please bird lovers.

RIDES AND FUN

Swing by any of Busch Gardens' "countries" to enjoy a plethora of rides, with choices for adults and children of all ages.

AERONAUT SKYRIDE ✪ Must See!

(England) Ride in cars and see all six countries of the park from high up in the sky. The enclosed individual coaches glide along cables reaching 80 feet in the air and stop in England, France, and Germany. They are a great way to get from one place to another especially at the end of a long day at the park.

ALPENGEIST

(Germany) Riders spiral 360 degrees and become completely inverted in a 106-foot vertical loop on this wild coaster named after a snow monster in the Alps. In fact, riders are inverted six times while dangling in ski-lift-style seats from the coaster's nearly 4,000 feet of steel track. This ride has consistently been voted one of the top ten steel coasters in the world since opening in 1997. That's most likely because of its non-stop action and crazy twists and turns. Speeds reach 67 mph during the two-minute and 30-second ride.

APOLLO'S CHARIOT

(Italy) You plunge a combined total of 825 feet on this wild coaster. That's more than on any other coaster in the world, according to the amusement park. Debuting in 1999, the coaster reaches speeds of 70 mph. The elevated seats create a free-fall effect, especially on the first dive which is 210 feet.

BATTERING RAM

(Italy) This ride is great for families as it's suitable for all ages, from walking children up, and family members can sit together on the same wide seat. This giant boat moves like a battering ram with seats on each half facing each other. It swings back and forth starting off slow, with each side gradually rising higher into the air until it feels like the boat is vertical. It's a thrill to feel weightless and fun to see riders screaming, laughing, and trying to hold on to their belongings. For maximum thrill, sit on the back row on either side. It's a good idea to secure loose items on this ride as your hands hold on to the bar in front of your seat.

EUROPE IN THE AIR

(Ireland) Guests become part of a breathtaking simulated journey into Europe in this high-tech ride. Through audio-visual magic and movement, they are transported across the terrain, seas and through the air to experience some of Europe's loveliest areas close-up.

CURSE OF DARKASTLE

(Germany) This is a good ride for families, with everyone sitting in the same sleigh. Keep in mind that children must be at least 42 inches tall to ride though. Guests wind through corridors of what looks like a real medieval castle as they wait in line. Then they enter a room and are shown a short film, which prepares them for the adventure ahead. Once in a sleigh, all kinds of special effects make it appear that objects and ghosts are whirling through the air. There's a good chance there will be a lot of screaming going on during this three-minute

20-second ride. It's a lot of fun, but can be a little scary, with objects sometimes appearing to fly directly at the riders, almost like weapons. Make sure children understand they're in no real danger.

DA VINCI'S CRADLE ✪ Must See!

(Italy) Riders sit in a large cradle with hinges that lift it up and then drop it back down quickly so they feel like they're going to hit the ground. The cradle then swings swiftly back up in the air lifting riders slightly off their seats. Riders should hold on tightly to eyeglasses, hats, and any other loose objects on this fun and choppy ride. It's great for groups or whole families as a lot of people can sit together on the cradle's bench-like seats.

DER AUTOBAHN

(Germany) This is Busch Gardens' version of classic bumper cars and can be fun for the whole family. There's a kid-friendly version nearby, **Der Autobahn Jr.,** for smaller "drivers."

ESCAPE FROM POMPEII

(Italy) This ride is a combination water ride and haunted house. Riders are seated in a large raft which travels up a ramp into a building. Here, various illusions give riders the sense of being in the midst of the fall of Pompeii. These include loud noises, fire, lava, and falling columns. After escaping the city, riders then come out the other side of the building and plummet steeply and quickly downhill into the lake where they will get quite wet. This ride can be fun for families or groups, but excludes children under 42 inches. It is a fun way to cool off in the summer.

GOIN' COUNTRY

(Canadian Pallidium, France) Guests are serenaded to country classics in this rustic, open-air theater near **Trappers Smokehouse**.

GRIFFON ✪ Must See!

(France) The park promotes its newest coaster Griffon as "the world's tallest and first floorless dive coaster." Because of the stadium-style seating with three rows of seats, riders feel like they are trackless. The ride begins with an initial 205-foot climb to the edge of a 90-degree drop. The ride abruptly stops there and riders dangle a few seconds before being dropped straight down at more than 70 mph. This take-your-breath-away drop is followed by a looping climb and another drop of 130 feet. It's the park's fastest coaster reaching 75 mph. Standing near **Bistro 205** in France will offer an awesome view of riders plunging down the first drop and going through the loop.

KINDER KARUSSEL

(Germany) Both the young and young at heart can take a ride on this beautifully restored antique Herschell Carousel. Riders can choose from 36 hand-carved ponies or ride in a lovely chariot seat.

LE SCOOT LOG FLUME ✪ Must See!

(France) A local favorite, the flume is a super way to cool off. Once settled in the log seat (each holds up to four riders), the flume slowly climbs high into the air via a ramp. Then following a series of dips and twists, riders end up inside a building which then opens to a long drop below. This drop is the best part of the ride, where riders usually get mildly wet to soaked. The ride is suitable for all ages, but children must at least be able to walk.

LOCH NESS MONSTER ✪ Must See!

(Scotland) A park and locals' favorite, this coaster has been at the park since it first opened over 30 years ago. According to park officials, it has traveled a distance equaling more than 150 trips around the world since that time. It was the world's first and is still the only interlocking, double-looping steel coaster.

From the first suspenseful climb and steep plunge that creates a feeling of being about to hit the water below, to twists, loops and turns, and scary dark tunnels, it's fun from start to finish.

PET SHENANIGANS

(Shenanigans Theatre, Ireland) This funny animal show features birds, dogs, cats, and other animals performing silly tricks.

ROMAN RAPIDS

(Italy) The giant round rafts of this ride each hold up to six riders. Riders are supposed to spin the raft and hold on using the wheel in the middle as the raft heads down a channel of rapids and waterfalls. Half the fun is in trying to turn the raft so riders on the opposite side get soaked, even while trying to dodge the waterfalls and sprays as the raft travels quickly along. Depending on where riders sit and how adept they are at spinning and dodging, they will get wet to varying degrees. It doesn't take long under one of the waterfalls to get soaked through and through. Riders must be at least 42 inches tall.

SESAME STREET PRESENTS LIGHTS, CAMERA IMAGINATION!

(Globe Theatre, England) This 4-D movie experience features Big Bird, Elmo, Cookie Monster, and other Sesame Street characters. It is suitable for all ages.

TURKISH DELIGHT

(Italy) Almost everyone can try this Busch Gardens' version of the spinning teacups. Sit in a life-sized cup alone or with a pal or two. Spin the wheel in the middle to turn the cup in different directions as it spins around and round. It starts off slower and then the speed increases; but slows down again at the end of the ride.

TRADEWIND

(Italy) This is a smaller ride which sits on a round raised track. One or two people sit in a car, and half the fun is pushing each other as the ride leans the seat one way, then the other as it spins quickly. This is a good transitional ride for a parent and older child to do together. It is especially good for children who are getting too big for the kiddie rides, but aren't quite ready for the big coasters yet. It's exciting enough for adults to enjoy too. Just remember not to carry anything in your pockets that you aren't prepared to squish.

TWEEDSIDE TRAIN STATION

(Scotland) Busch Gardens' three locomotives provide a nice change of pace, allowing guests to sit back, relax, and enjoy the park from a different perspective. Children usually enjoy riding the trains which wind through 200 acres of the park. Guests traveling the track's entire loop will cross the "Rhine River" on a tall bridge between Scotland and France. The trains are an easy way to get from one country to the other when station lines are not too long. Besides Scotland, the trains stop in Italy and France.

ESPECIALLY FOR LITTLE ONES

There are two large play areas at the park designed especially for small children, **Land of the Dragons** and the **Sesame Street Forest of Fun**. In general, these are great places for parents and children alike. They are not gated, but there's only one way in and out so it's easier for parents to watch children. This allows parents to relax a little and gives children more independence than in other areas of the park because everything is just their size. Both areas feature entertainment and free play areas for children to use their imaginations and burn off some energy.

Besides these two play areas, there is a special dining room where children can eat with Elmo and Friends. This is located in **Castle O'Sullivan** in Ireland and was new to the park in 2009. Children can visit with costumed characters in this Sesame Street-themed restaurant while they enjoy a meal. The buffet-style restaurant serves chicken tenders, macaroni and cheese, hot dogs, barbecued chicken, cheesy hash browns and other kids' favorites. There is also a 4-D movie with Sesame Street characters in England's **Globe Theater**.

Besides the special areas mentioned above, there are rides throughout the park designed for smaller children. Many of these are concentrated in the area between **Das Festhaus** in Germany moving toward Italy. In Germany guests will find kiddie plane and swing rides plus junior bumper cars. Cross the bridge into Italy and just past San Marcos there are more children's rides. These include mini-balloon and glider rides plus **Elephant Run**. This is a child's version of the grown-up's **Tradewind**. The two large play areas are described in more detail here.

LAND OF THE DRAGONS

(Germany) This dragon-themed area is packed with rides, a three-story treehouse with slides, giant dragon eggs, and lots of other places to play. The dragons here are very cute and not the least bit scary. Parents can accompany children on two of the area's rides. One is Eggery Deggery, a Ferris wheel with seats shaped liked giant dragon eggs. The other is Flutter Sputter, where riders can sit inside a dragon which "flies" up in the air in circles. Rides for kids only include a kiddie boat ride called Chug-a-Tug and a lady bug "car" ride called Bug-A-Dug. There is a dragon-themed open-air show for kids. If parents need a break, there are lots of places to sit and relax while kids play.

SESAME STREET FOREST OF FUN

(England) This is a new attraction introduced in 2009. It is a special fun area just for kids located between England and Italy. It features popular Sesame Street characters. The area has family-friendly rides like Grover's Alpine Express, a mini coaster, and Prince Elmo's Spire, which takes riders straight up and down on a platform. Adults may also accompany children on Oscar's Whirly Worms and a miniature flume ride, Bert and Ernie's Loch Adventure.

Children can have fun exploring wet and dry play areas here. Elmo's Castle is a wet play area where children can wade through shallow pools and run through spraying jets of water.

It includes an interactive stage with costumed characters. Children can have fun without getting wet in Oscar's Yucky Forest. Parents can capture their child's fun day here by having their photo taken with their favorite Sesame Street character at 1-2-3 Smile With Me!

RESTAURANTS

No matter what part of the park you're in, there is always a place nearby to grab a quick snack and drink, or even a sit-down meal. There are lots of outdoor snack kiosks (too many to mention) serving à la carte items, and everything from smoked turkey legs to Budweiser lime-grilled shrimp. There are a few places that offer indoor dining, including **Das Festhaus** where you can watch a live show while you eat. Most of the restaurants though, are cafeteria-style. Walk through a line, make your selections, take the tray, and pay. You can dine on tables outdoors. Most of the larger restaurants offer kids' meals.

Many of the restaurants here serve some of the same items. The same pizza and cherry chocolate cake, for example, can be found at multiple locations throughout the park. Many also serve Anheuser-Busch beers on tap. These include Budweiser, Bud Light, Michelob Ultra, and O'Doul's. A few, including **Ristorante della Piazza**, serve a small selection of wines. **Grogan's Pub** in Ireland serves other alcoholic beverages as well.

As there are too many food outlets to mention them all, this section highlights those offering foods authentic to the "country" where they are located, as well as park favorites.

BISTRO 205

(France) Eat to your heart's content at this buffet-style restaurant. Try pulled pork barbecue, fried chicken, hot dogs, macaroni and cheese, tortellini in butter sauce, mixed vegetables, French fries, and garlic potatoes. There is also a salad bar and a choice of assorted desserts. Adults can eat for around $15 and children between 3–9 years for approximately $10.

CAFÉ LULU

(New France) This small shop serves snack items like smoked turkey legs wrapped in foil to take on the go, corn dogs, nachos, pretzels, drinks, and fruit smoothies. Fresh churros with sugar and cinnamon are also sold here.

DAS FESTHAUS ✪ Must See!

(Germany) Everything is big here, from the food to the festivities. Get the experience of Oktoberfest while dining indoors at long wooden tables in this large hall which holds 2,000 guests. Regular shows take place on the raised platform in the middle of the hall where entertainers in German costumes sing and dance. Be prepared to get up and dance as they may try to recruit you to join in. Expect delicious food and large portions great for big appetites. The Das Alpine is a great meal which can almost be shared by two. It is a tall, multi-layered corn beef and Swiss sandwich on rye, served with German potato salad. Other specialty items on the menu include red cabbage, authentic German sausages, and German chocolate cake. This is a fun place well worth a visit, but probably not for a quiet dining experience away from the crowds.

DINE AT CASTLE O'SULLIVAN

(Ireland) Little ones can dine with Elmo and Friends at this dining hall in Ireland.

GROGAN'S GRILL

(Ireland) Sample Irish comfort foods at this restaurant that offers outdoor dining only. Options include Irish stew served in a fresh-baked soda bread bowl for around $8 or one of several sampler platters. The Irish Sample Patter includes stew, seasoned pork loin, and cheesy hash browns for around $10.

LA CUCINA

(Italy) Located near the **Roman Rapids**, this cafeteria-style restaurant sells gourmet burgers, wraps, pizza, and other items, with pretty much everything under $10.

M. SWEETS CONFECTIONARY

(Banbury Cross) Guests will find all kinds of mouth-watering sweets in this shop. It sells cake by the slice, strudel, cookies, an ample selection of fudges, hand-dipped pretzels, plus more. Try a gourmet apple covered in nuts, chocolates and sprinkles, candies, or caramel with the basic candied apple priced around $5. The shop also sells brand-name candies like Jelly Belly pre-packaged or by the pound.

PIGS IN A KILT

(Scotland) If you're a hot dog fan, you might want to try a hand dipped corn dog at this dine-out restaurant near **Heatherdowns**. It also serves chicken tenders, fries, sodas, and lemonade.

RISTORANTE DELLA PIAZZA

(Italy) This is the place to dine for traditional Italian dishes. The restaurant serves everything from Canneloni alla Stella to spaghetti with marinara sauce. Most items fall in the $8 to $10 range, and a kid's meal is around a dollar less. Anheuser-Busch products are available on tap.

SQUIRE'S GRILLE

(England) This restaurant is close to the **Big Ben** replica near the park entrance. It serves breakfast and lunch. It is open all day right to a half-hour past the park's closing. The location and hours make it convenient for grabbing something quickly on the way in or out of the park. Diners have to walk through a cafeteria-style line to order and then can dine outside at umbrella-covered tables. For breakfast, the restaurant serves English muffins, eggs, pan potatoes, waffles, fresh fruits, and oven-baked pastries. Lunch includes pizza slices, wraps, burgers, and chicken tenders. Some items are served with homemade chips and others with French fries. Most items are in the $7–8 range. Anheuser-Busch beers are available here, including Budweiser, Bud Light, Michelob Ultra, and O'Doul's. If you have more of a sweet tooth or just want a quick snack, a shop adjacent to the Grille sells funnel cakes with toppings like fresh strawberries. To the other side, the London Dairy dishes out soft-serve ice cream.

THREE RIVERS SNACKS

(France) Guests can buy kettle corn, funnel cakes, and Anheuser-Busch beer at this snack stop. Take it on the go or sit outside on a rustic, split-log bench.

TRAPPERS SMOKEHOUSE

(France) This restaurant caters to fans of outdoor grilling and smoking. It offers smoked beef brisket and barbecued chicken and baby back ribs, grilled salmon, and lots more. Side items include slaw, mixed green salad, corn-on-the-cob, baked beans, and macaroni and cheese. Desserts range from ample slices of chocolate cherry cake to fresh-cut watermelon. Anheuser-Busch beverages are sold here too. You walk through an indoor cafeteria line and dine outside on rustic tables or benches.

SHOPPING

There are shops and kiosks all over **Busch Gardens**. A great many of these sell basic souvenir items like tee-shirts, sunglasses, cups, and children's items. However, there are many shops that sell specialty items as well. Since there are too many shops to include them all here, this section highlights those which sell unusual or specialty items not available everywhere.

ALPENGEIST GIFTS

(Germany) This small, open-air shop sells Volcom skate apparel and accessories, plus Vans shoes. A pair of Volcom shorts sells for about $50.

ARTISANS OF ITALY

(Italy) This open-air shop sells fine Italian items, yet there is something for every budget. A necklace with a porcelain flower pendant can be purchased for under $20 or a Gallo clock for more than a thousand. They have a nice selection of Capodimonte porcelain items.

THE BEAR'S PAW

(France) Guests can have a personalized wooden sign made for their home at this small shop on the outskirts of New France. Choose from a variety of styles.

BELLA CASA

(Italy) This is a small open-air store near the **Teatro di San Marco**. The most beautiful hand-painted Venetian masks available here come in a variety of sizes, colors, and designs. They are made in Italy and well worth checking out.

CARIBOU POTTERY

(France) A pretty piece of glazed pottery or a fine dinnerware piece can be bought in this shop which looks like a log cabin. There are fun hands-on opportunities as well which include painting a piece of pottery that you choose from a large selection of unfinished pieces. Shoppers can even dip a candle. This is an affordable option for letting little ones be creative, and the candles come in fun designs like frogs, turtles, and dinosaurs. They range in price from $4 to $10 based on size. Just pick and pay for the candle of choice, begin dipping in assorted colors, and get the candle wrapped at the counter when it's finished.

DAS STEIN HAUS ✪ Must See!

(Germany) This shop sells beautiful handcrafted steins with lids or without, including limited editions. It also offers nutcrackers and Bavarian clocks. There's a Christmas room in the rear of the shop that's worth a visit, even if just to experience the wonderful smells. A large tree here displays ornaments, while other holiday items line the walls. Santa Claus here comes in a variety of styles and sizes, some several feet tall.

EMERALD ISLE GIFTS

(Ireland) This shop sells fine crystal goblets, lamps, and vases. Also available here are beautiful pure wool sweaters made in Ireland which run around $65. A fine Irish men's wool hat can be yours for a little less. For those looking to spend even less cash, the store sells some less expensive items like Irish penny whistles for around $15.

LA BELLE MAISON

(France) This is a small, upscale clothing shop selling Quiksilver shorts, tee-shirts and shoes, Vans shoes, and Roxy clothing, wallets, handbags, and watches. You can also find handcrafted woven bags by Scala for around $50 or take home a Scala hat for around half that. This shop also sells costume jewelry and designer sunglasses.

THE OYSTER'S SECRET

(France) Also called Le Secret De l'Ocean, this small shop sells fine gold, silver, and pearl jewelry, as well as costume jewelry. Outside near the entrance, shoppers can pick their very own oyster containing an Akoya pearl from a shallow tank for under $20, and buy it as is or purchase the perfect setting for the gem inside the shop. The shop also sells beautiful Mad by Design shell and horn handbags starting around $40.

POT O' GOLD

(Ireland) Magic rules in this shop, which is loaded with magic toys and tricks, dragons galore, gargoyles, and more. For those intrigued by dragons, the shop has a large selection of figurines, toys, books, and shirts bearing the fire-breathing reptiles. There are even hand-carved dragon hiking sticks which cost $30. Magic tricks start around $3.

TOYS O' THE LEPRECHAUN ✪ Must See!

(Ireland) Children and adults alike will most likely love browsing through this whimsical shop where fantasy comes first. For families with "little princesses," there are fairy-dust necklaces, wands, princess dresses, and tiaras. Little boys can find costumes and accessories to dress up like a real medieval knight. The shop also sells a large selection of plush toys and Golden Keepsakes dolls.

TRADING POST AND TOBACCO CO.

(France) This shop sells lots of items commemorating frontier life, including replica swords and guns, and faux coonskin caps. Guests can choose from a large selection of beautiful hand-made Native American dolls. They can also purchase a feath-ered headdress made on the Qualla reservation in Cherokee, North Carolina. For children the shop sells old-fashioned wooden toys, toy guns, swords, and bow-and-arrow sets.

CHRISTMAS TOWN

For the holidays, **Busch Gardens** is totally transformed in the evenings into a beautifully lit wonderland called Christmas Town. Each European village of the park is tastefully decorated in a different theme of lights, trees, greenery, and bows, with music to match. Ireland features green lights, for example, and the French village has pretty pastel lights and trees. Lighted snowflakes hang in the sky in some places in the park, and in others, snow falls from the sky. Carolers sing in the streets in some areas.

To give the senses a break, walkways in between each village are more serene. They are low-lit by solid-colored lights on hundreds of trees in the landscape along the walkways. On some paths, lighted stars hang above the trees. Approximately a million and a half lights illuminate the entire park, including the 45-foot Christmas tree in Germany. Every half hour, the tree bursts into an amazing light and musical *O Tannebaum* show.

Christmas Town is for all ages and offers an ideal opportunity for family members to reconnect during the holiday season. The **Griffon** roller coaster is open for older children and adults in France, as is the carousel and several other rides in the park. The train, all decorated for the holidays, also runs between France and England.

There are also many special activities for small children. They can dine with Santa in Ireland at "Santa's Fireside Feast." In Germany they can have their photos taken with Santa in "Santa's Workshop" at the "North Pole." A "Sesame Street Christmas" show in England's **Globe Theater** features an array of Sesame Street characters who discover the meaning of Christmas.

A live orchestra and chorus perform *Rejoice*, a more traditional Christmas concert, in the park's **Abbey Stone Theatre** in Ireland. **Das Festhaus** in Germany features a rousing, colorful Broadway-style *Deck the Halls* show all ages can enjoy while dining on a traditional turkey dinner and other hot meals. Restaurants and snack carts throughout the park feature warm foods and beverages like soups, stews, s'mores, and hot cocoa. There's even red, white, and green kettle corn. **Grogan's Pub** in Ireland offers hot toddies and festive cocktails.

There's an outdoor market featuring approximately 40 artists and vendors from the area and beyond. This **Mistletoe Marketplace** is located in Germany. Shoppers here will find items like beautiful glass pieces made at Jamestown, hand-sewn purses, handcrafted jewelry, and much more.

Shops throughout the park sell holiday and seasonal items like holiday wreaths, books, ornaments, plush Santas, snowmen, and bears. There are also many Christmas Town souvenirs like shirts and mugs, which can be personalized with names. A scale model of **Griffon** is also available that can be put together for about $100. To memorialize a visit to Christmas Town, visitors can dress in costumes for a photo in a festive antique sleigh in a snow scene.

To keep guests warm while visiting Christmas Town, the park has raised heaters on stands in some areas. There are also heated tents for comfortable outdoor dining.

Admission to Christmas Town is around $20 for adults. There is also a $10 parking fee per car, but you can save a couple dollars by purchasing this in advance online. Quick Queue tickets can be purchased inside the park for an additional $15 or so. These can automatically get you to the front of some lines, reserved seating to shows, and express access to Santa.

Christmas Town runs from the weekend following Thanksgiving to New Year's Eve on Fridays through Sundays, plus several additional days close to Christmas Day. The park opens for the attraction in the late afternoons around 3:00 p.m. The park is closed on Christmas Day.

ACCOMMODATIONS NEAR BUSCH GARDENS

The places listed here are within a five-minute drive of Busch Gardens. This also makes them close to the other two parks, **Water Country USA** and **President's Park**. They are ideal places to stay if your main reason for visiting Williamsburg is to spend the maximum amount of time at the theme parks.

They are also in a location which will make it easy to find the way to Yorktown. Keep in mind also that Colonial Williamsburg is within ten minutes of Busch Gardens and the major outlets shops are only about ten minutes farther away. The hotels listed below are within a short driving distance of pretty much everything the area has to offer.

Having said that, the hotels listed here are by no means the only places to stay while visiting Busch Gardens. Almost all of the hotels named in this book are within a half-hour drive of all the sights and attractions that Williamsburg has to offer.

Standard room rate in peak season starts at under $100 = ($), $100-$200 = ($$), and above $200 = ($$$).

COURTYARD BY MARRIOTT WILLIAMSBURG

(470 McLaws Circle ☎ 757.221.0700 🖳 marriott.com) This *AAA Three Diamond* hotel is close to all the theme parks. It has four floors and has large indoor and outdoor pool areas which connect, as well as a hot tub. There is also a café offering a daily breakfast buffet and a restaurant which serves dinner. Rooms and suites, which include living rooms, are simple yet bright. They include refrigerators, high-speed Internet, ergonomically-designed chairs, and premium-cable television. It is a non-smoking and non-pet hotel. *($$)*

DAYS HOTEL WILLIAMSBURG

(201 Water Country Parkway ☎ 757.253.6444 ☗ daysinn.com)
This multi-story budget hotel is adjacent to **President's Park**
and only a couple minutes from **Busch Gardens** and **Water
Country USA**. It's an inexpensive option for visitors interested primarily in being close to the theme parks. Rooms are
modern and include televisions with HBO, hair dryers, irons
and ironing boards, and DVD players. Site amenities include
a game room, outdoor pool, playground, picnic area, and
a 24-hour fitness center. There is a restaurant, but it serves
breakfast only and only on weekends during the off season.
No pets are allowed. *($)*

KINGSMILL RESORT AND SPA

(1010 Kingsmill Rd. ☎ 757.253.1703 ☗ kingsmill.com) This
lovely resort is located along the James River adjacent to
Busch Gardens and offers guests a free shuttle to the theme
park and other area attractions. It is the largest golf resort
in Virginia. It features three world-class golf courses, several
restaurants, a full-service spa, large tennis complex, and state-
of-the-art fitness center. There are also indoor and outdoor
pools, a game room, a gift shop, and many complimentary
activities including camps and programs for children. Choose
villas with either one, two, or three bedrooms. Standard rooms
include a private balcony or patio, desks, wireless Internet,
and cable television. Golf packages are available. No pets are
allowed here. *($$)*

QUALITY INN AT KINGSMILL

(480 McLaws Circle ☎ 757.220.1100

✆ qualityinn.com) This three-story hotel is about five minutes from **Busch Gardens, Water Country USA**, and **President's Park**. It has good amenities for the price. Guests get a free complimentary breakfast. There's also a game room, outdoor pool and an indoor pool housed in an atrium-style room, and free high-speed Internet access in public areas. The rooms are somewhat plain but clean. They include satellite television, Internet access, hair dryers, and irons and ironing boards with refrigerators and microwaves available upon request. No smoking or pets are permitted. *($$)*

WILLIAMSBURG MARRIOTT

(50 Kingsmill Rd. ☎ 757.220.2500 ✆ marriott.com) This *AAA Three Diamond* hotel is very close to **Busch Gardens**. Guests get free wireless Internet in community areas and guest rooms and suites. Rooms include special touches like down pillows. There are connecting indoor and outdoor pools, a whirlpool, and fitness center. There's a restaurant and a bar/lounge. No pets or smoking is allowed. *($$)*

Colonial Williamsburg is the largest living history museum in the country and is a primary source of knowledge on colonial life in America.

Activities in the Williamsburg Area

Apart from visiting theme parks, there are various other activities for you to try while in town. These range from water parks to a relaxing salt spa experience. Try one or try them all.

AMF WILLIAMSBURG LANES

(5544 Olde Towne Rd. ☎ 757.565.3311) This large bowling alley has 40 lanes and hosts the Colonial Virginia Tournament. The alley offers both bumper and extreme bowling. There is a snack bar where you can grab a bite to eat, and also a full bar. The alley stays open daily and on Fridays and Saturdays, it's open late until 1:00 a.m.

COLONIAL DOWNS RACETRACK

(10515 Colonial Downs Parkway, New Kent ☎ 804.966.7223 🖰 colonialdowns.com) This is Virginia's only pari-mutuel horseracing track. It is located just west of Williamsburg in neighboring New Kent County just off I-64 (Exit 214). The track holds thoroughbred racing in the summer and harness races in the fall. It also offers special activities like a fireworks celebration on the 4th of July.

The track has a family-friendly environment and can be a lot of fun for young and old alike. Kids usually enjoy seeing the horses before and during the races. The horses are paraded around a viewing area, often by their jockeys, before each race so that those placing wagers can get a good look at them.

Colonial Downs' annual showcase event is the Virginia Derby and is broadcast on national television in July. Another popular event is the Colonial Turf Cup held about four weeks before the derby.

The venue's Secretariat Turf Course is the widest grass surface of any track in North America. Its one-and-a-quarter-mile dirt track is the country's second largest next to Belmont's. The dirt track allows harness horses to pace or trot a one-mile distance while maneuvering only one turn. This is the only track anywhere to offer this unique configuration, according to Colonial Downs.

The track has several places to eat. There are outdoor concession stands which offer items like Philly cheesesteaks, Italian sausage sandwiches, chicken nuggets, fries, lemonade, and sodas. Indoor first-floor concessions offer additional items like pizza, burgers, ice cream, pretzels, and popcorn.

The Turf and Jockey clubs upstairs offer full meals and a balcony view of the races. Reservations are recommended for both and advance reservations require a minimum of four persons. Seating in these areas runs a little higher than the general admission price. The track also has Sky Suite packages for those wanting a top-of-the-line experience including a lush suite and several-course meal. There is a 15-person minimum for these accommodations though.

General admission is only a couple of bucks per person, with free entry for children 12 years and under. Grandstand and other seating options are also available. A racing program runs a few dollars more, but is a must-have for anyone planning to place wagers. You must be 18 years or older to bet at the track.

GO-KARTS PLUS
(6910 Richmond Rd. ☎ 757.564.7600 ▮ gokartsplus.com)
Located near the **Williamsburg Pottery**, this small amusement park offers fun rides for both children and adults, especially

anyone who's ever dreamed of being a race car driver. Because it's small, visitors can spend more time participating in activities and less time walking from place to place or waiting in lines. The park includes several styles of mini racing cars like Formula One racers and three large tracks, plus a "rookie" track for smaller children. There are bumper cars and boats, which allow you to squirt water at other boaters while maneuvering inside a pool. The miniature golf course has 18 holes, and there's also a basketball shootout area. The indoor arcade is great for when it is really hot out or rainy. There is a snack bar and a covered picnic pavilion. The park stays open daily from June through August, with reduced hours in the spring beginning in mid-March and in the fall through October. Admission and parking is free, but visitors have to pay per ride.

HAUNTED DINNER THEATER

(5363 Richmond Rd. ☎ 757.258.2500
🖱 haunteddinnertheater.com) This theater is located in **Captain George's Seafood Restaurant**. Participate as little or as much as you like in this interactive theatrical experience which takes place while you dine on plates of food from the 70-plus-item buffet at Captain George's. You'll get the chance to help solve a mystery in an exciting performance like "Shipwrecked in Williamsburg." The experience is family-friendly and fun but not scary. Tickets run around $45 for adults and a little under $30 for children between 5–12 years, with children under 4 free. Tickets can be reserved by phone or online.

OASIS OF WILLIAMSBURG

(1915 Pocahontas Trail Suite A7 ☎ 757.229.9430
🖱 oasisofwilliamsburg.com) This day spa is located at the **Village Shops** at **Kingsmill**. It offers a variety of facials,

body treatments, and massages. Massages range from a simple 10-minute chair massage to hot stone, deep tissue, and Swedish massages. There's even a prenatal massage for expectant mothers. The spa also offers nail, tanning, and hair-removal services. Walk-ins are welcome for most services, but appointments are recommended and Sundays are by appointment only. The spa is open Mondays through Saturdays.

PIRATE'S COVE ADVENTURE GOLF

(**2001 Mooretown Rd.** ☎ **757.259.4600** 🖱 **piratescove.com**) This well-maintained 18-hole miniature golf course can be fun for all ages. It includes waterfalls, mountain caves, and footbridges. It is centrally located off Bypass Road near the Dairy Queen.

PRESIDENT'S PARK

(**211 Water Country Pkwy.** ☎ **757.259.1121**

🖱 **presidentspark.org**) Did you know that James Madison was only five foot, four inches tall? Or that Jimmy Carter pardoned 10,000 Vietnam War draft evaders his first day as president? Learn interesting facts about all the U.S. presidents at this indoor-outdoor attraction. Move along an outdoor walkway to see large busts of the 42 men who've served as U.S. presidents. Each statue stands 16- to 18-feet tall and weighs about 7,500 pounds. A small prototype of President Barack Obama's statue is set up inside the museum, although his large bust hadn't yet been added in 2009. The park was reportedly still raising the $60,000 needed for the statue. Internationally acclaimed artist David Adickes created all the park's statues.

Each statue is accompanied by plaques with biographical information such as when and where each president was born. Walk from statue to statue and read as much – or as little – information as you choose. There are also 14 signs documenting defining moments in American history, such as the Civil Rights Movement. Some of these have audio buttons to hear more information.

Inside the two-story museum is the **First Lady's Tea Parlor**. It's a pretty small dining area, but there is also additional seating outside on the patio during nice weather. You can have a light lunch or tea and a dessert like sweet potato pie. The parlor offers many tasty teas in flavors like ginger peach or white pear. It also serves delicious sandwiches including a delectable cranberry chicken salad on raisin bread. The recipes for the baked items and sandwiches are created by manager Jerri Burrell and KJ Jordan.

In addition to managing the tea parlor, Burrell also designs the first ladies' dresses on display in the lobby downstairs. A movie on the American presidency is shown there. Plus, there is an oval office replica. You can take pictures seated in the office or with life-size cutouts of Barack or Michelle Obama and others at a minimal cost. A gift shop sells some unusual items. You can buy famous speeches by Patrick Henry and others printed on parchment paper.

There are also campaign buttons, prints, and books on the presidents, as well as some of the first ladies. The shop also sells some Virginia and Williamsburg souvenirs, all pretty reasonably priced. A nice companion book to the park that includes information on all the presidents can be purchased for about $13.

Upstairs, there is a small exhibit on presidential pets, and an observation deck where you can get a nice view of the park. There is also a documentary on Barack Obama's life played here.

Admission is a little over $12 for adults and $8 for children between 6 and 12 years.

RIPLEY'S BELIEVE IT OR NOT! MUSEUM
(1735 Richmond Rd. ☎ 757.220.9220
🖱 williamsburgripleys.com) This museum is very interesting and features many interactive and exotic exhibits. It has more than 300 items on display, highlighting the "weird and wonderful," and offering something to interest all ages. There are life-size replicas of real people, science exhibits, and displays set in natural disasters, the jungle, and other places. Some highlight foreign and obscure cultures. Some exhibits feature cool special effects, like the colorful walk-through vortex tunnels. Some of the displays are a bit grotesque. The museum's theatre shows fun 3-D movies with 4-D effects, surround sound, and simulation effects. The seats move in eight different directions. The museum stays open daily, and keeps reduced hours on some holidays like Thanksgiving and Christmas Day. Theater and museum admission can be purchased separately or there are several combination tickets which include both. A combination of one trip to the museum and one feature in the theater runs close to $23 for an adult when purchased at the site. Admission for 5-12 year olds is a little cheaper and those 4 and under get in free. It's very worthwhile for guests to purchase tickets online to save about $2 off each ticket.

WATER COUNTRY USA
(176 Water Country Pkwy. ☎ 800.343.7946
🖱 watercountryusa.com) Celebrating its 26th year, this is the Mid-Atlantic's largest water park featuring more than 30 water slides, rides, and attractions. With its upbeat '50s and '60s surf theme, this can be a great place for the entire family to cool off

and enjoy a splash. It is located very close to **Busch Gardens** and is operated by the same company, Sea World Parks and Entertainment owned by Blackstone. The newest park addition is "Rock 'n' Roll Island" which opened in 2008. It features three body slides, each close to 200-feet long, which empty into a 9,000-square-foot pool. For little ones, the island has a "Little Bopper" slide.

Visitors can basically get as adventurous as they want. There are gentler areas appropriate for all ages, sizes, and swimming levels, like the shallow part of Surfer's Bay, a 23,000-square-foot pool with waves that simulate the ocean. Then there are wilder rides like Malibu Pipeline, 468-foot-long tubes winding through waterfalls and darkness before emptying into a three-foot-deep splash pool.

With safety in mind, there are various height and age requirements for each ride, plus different recommendations for wearing life vests. In Surfer's Bay, for example, weak or non-swimmers are asked not to venture beyond a certain point without a life vest, as the water reaches depths of eight feet. Also, for some rides, like the Big Daddy Falls, children must be accompanied by a "supervisory companion" at least 14 years old.

There are great opportunities for adults and children to interact on rides like the parent/child slide in the H2O UFO area, where a parent and child get on a 42-inch tube together. This area also has children's slides, a semi-submerged tunnel, a tire swing, water guns, wheels, and fountains.

For those who don't want to get wet at all, there are 1,500 lounge chairs for sunbathing or just relaxing. There are also 16 private cabanas available for rent throughout the park.

While wearing bathing suits or shorts is fine, thongs are not allowed, and tee-shirts cannot be worn on body flumes. Swim diapers are required in some areas for children in that age group. These are available for $2 from vending machines in the park. Life vests and inner tubes are complimentary.

There are plenty of facilities for bathing and changing on the site. There are also baby-changing stations in all the children's areas. Lockers can be rented for storing personal items.

You can really settle in for the day here as there are seven places to eat on-site, as well as surf and gift shops.

Open the end of May through beginning of September, the water park has a general one-day admission of just over $40 for adults, around $35 for 3-9 year olds, and is free for children under 3. Combination **Busch Gardens** tickets are also available, as are multi-day passes.

WILLIAMSBURG SALT SPA
(1111 Old Colony Ln. ☎ 757.229.1022

● williamsburgsaltspa.com) Relax and rejuvenate in this salt cave created from 15 tons of salt imported from Pakistan and Poland. Salt caves have been used for centuries for therapeutic reasons. Spa goers sit in reclining lounge chairs in the low-lit cave for 45-minute sessions. Sessions can be either private or public. In a public session, you sit in the cave with others who've scheduled a treatment. In a private session, your party (up to eight people) can book the cave. A public session runs around $25 per adult, with discounted rates offered for seniors and children. The salt spa is open Mondays through Saturdays. Call in advance to schedule an appointment.

THE WILLIAMSBURG WINERY, LTD.

(5800 Wessex Hundred ☎ 757.229.0999

williamsburgwinery.com) Established in 1985, this is Virginia's largest winery. It has won many awards, especially for its white wines, and produces more than 60,000 cases of wine annually. That is about a quarter of the total wine produced in the commonwealth each year. The winery has more than 50 acres of vineyards and produces over a dozen wines. Its Governors White, a fruity semi-dry blend is its best seller and in fact, the best-selling white wine in Virginia. And among other awards, its John Adlum Chardonnay was recently named a "Best Buy" by *Wine Enthusiast.* The winery's **Gabriel Archer Tavern** has a pretty view of the grounds and serves lunch daily and dinner Thursdays through Mondays. Dinner is not served January through early April. Reservations are suggested. Visitors can stay overnight at the winery in its luxurious European-style hotel, **Wedmore Place**. It features three large luxury suites and 25 rooms ranging from traditional to superior. All are decorated with antiques and have wood-burning fireplaces. The winery is open daily for tours and tastings. There's also a nice wine shop that sells all sorts of wine-related accessories, plus gourmet sauces, spreads, and treats. *($$$)*

Colonial Williamsburg has more than 70 artisans who practice colonial trades and crafts at 21 sites in the Historic Area.

Restaurants in the Area

There are hundreds and hundreds of places to dine in the Greater Williamsburg area. Visitors will find all the well-known chains from fast-food restaurants like the Sonic drive-in and Hardee's, to sit-down places like **Cracker Barrel**, **Outback Steakhouse**, **TGI Friday's**, **Olive Garden**, and **Red Lobster**. Many of these restaurants serve good food. Therefore, if you're in the mood to dine on what is familiar and comfortable, then you will likely find your favorite place here.

There are many opportunities to try one-of-kind establishments or small independent chains though. We highly recommend that visitors try as many of these as possible. There really is something here for every budget.

Diners can try a pulled pork barbecue sandwich at the famous **Pierce's Pitt Bar-b-que** for under $5 or for a couple dollars more, try a loaded sub from the **New York Deli**. For something trendy and unique, consider a meal at **Food for Thought**. If you're in the mood for a big juicy steak, visit the **Aberdeen Barn**. Or for an elegant evening out for two, **Le Yaca** is a good choice.

This section primarily highlights restaurants that are unique or very popular here, whether it be for the great food or atmosphere, or both. There are simply too many good dining establishments in the area to mention them all so the restaurants listed below provide a broad sampling of the various types of cuisine and the dining environments offered. Some restaurants in the area are listed in other sections of this book as well. Restaurants within Colonial Williamsburg's Historic Area, for example, are already mentioned in that chapter.

The scale for the dinner entrées is as follows: under \$10 = (\$), \$10-\$20 = (\$\$), and above \$20 = (\$\$\$).

CASUAL DINING

If you are looking to dine in a casual setting, where the focus is on food, head to any of the places listed below.

COFFEE BEANERY CAFÉ

(1303 Jamestown Rd. Colony Square Shopping Center ☎ 757.258.2600) This coffeeshop sells breakfast and lunch besides a large selection of hot and cold beverages. Breakfast items are very reasonably priced and range from croissants and bagel sandwiches to crumb cakes and muffins. For lunch, choose from deli sandwiches, wraps, panini, soups, and salads. The café also sells pies, cakes, brownies, and other sweets. There's plenty of seating and free Internet access. *(\$)*

EMERALD THAI

(264 Mclaws Circle #G ☎ 757.645.2511 ☗ emeraldthaicuisine.com) Diners here can expect excellent Thai fare served by a courteous, friendly staff. The prices are also reasonable. The restaurant stays open daily. *(\$)*

FIVE FORKS CAFÉ

(4456 John Tyler Hwy. ☎ 757.221.0484 ☗ fiveforkscafe.com) This restaurant serves good home-cooked food. It has the look and feel of an old-fashioned diner, with its unassuming exterior, metallic tables and window booths in the dining area. They offer breakfast and lunch, and recently began serving dinner. There's a blue plate special menu good from 3:00 to 5:00 p.m. It is open daily except Mondays. *(\$)*

JIMMY'S OVEN & GRILL

(7201 Richmond Rd. ☎ 757.565.1465 🖰 jimmysovenandgrill.com)
This casual family-style restaurant has been open for more
than 30 years for good reason. Located at Norge, it offers
very good food at reasonable prices. The friendly staff serves
up great handmade pizzas. The soups are also very popular,
including the corn chowder, tomato bisque, and Chesapeake
clam chowder. They have daily specials on weekdays, an award-
winning seafood buffet on Fridays, and a prime rib special on
Saturdays. On Sundays, brunch is offered, but on other days,
the restaurant is open for lunch and dinner only. There's also a
full bar. The restaurant is open daily, except Thanksgiving and
Christmas Day. *($$)*

NATIONAL PANCAKE HOUSE

(1605 Richmond Rd. ☎ 757.220.5542) You can get a delicious
breakfast all day at this pancake house. The food is fresh and
the staff friendly. *($)*

NEW YORK DELI & PIZZA RESTAURANT

(6546 Richmond Rd. ☎ 757.564.9258 🖰 newyorkdelipizza.com)
No one should leave here hungry. This popular local deli-
style restaurant serves super sandwiches and subs, plus gyros,
souvlaki, salads, Stromboli, pizza, and traditional Italian dishes.
The portions are very large and the food tastes fresh. There are
more than 40 sub and sandwich choices on the menu like the
Chandler with roast beef, bacon, Swiss cheese, lettuce, tomato,
and mayo piled high on a sub roll. Sides range from hummus
with pita to Monterey jack poppers. Desserts include New
York cheesecake, walnut baklava, pecan pie, and other selec-
tions. Children can eat for around $4. Wine is sold by the glass
and you can get bottled or draft beer. The dining area is open

and casual with flat screen televisions on the walls for viewing and Louis Armstrong singing Hello Dolly or soft jazz playing in the background. Open Tuesdays through Sundays. *($)*

PAUL'S DELI RESTAURANT
(761 Scotland St. ☎ 757.229.8976

☗ paulsdelirestaurant.com) This deli has been recognized regionally by the *Virginia Gazette* as well as nationally in *Rolling Stone* magazine as one of the best delis in the country. It offers sit-down meals in booths and at tables in a diner-like eating area. The large menu includes subs, Stromboli, pizza, soups, quiche, fried dinner platters, and many other Italian, Greek, and American selections. Desserts range from pecan pie to homemade baklava. The sports bar is a casual fun place to hang out in the evenings. It has ten plasma televisions and offers beer on tap and bottled. A large selection of drinks and shooters are also mixed here. It stays open daily until late. *($)*

PIERCE'S PITT BAR B-QUE
(447 East Rochambeau ☎ 757.565.2955 ☗ pierces.com) This famous barbecue restaurant is a couple miles off the beaten path, but highly recommended to anyone who likes a good barbecue sandwich. Diners here will join the ranks of some well-known Virginia politicians like Senator Mark Warner, former Governor Tim Kaine, and former Senator John Warner. It has earned many awards for its barbecue since opening in 1971, but the most popular dish is its pulled pork barbecue marinated in its Pierce's original sauce. The recipe for this sweet and tangy red sauce was brought to Virginia from Flat Creek, Tennessee, by "Doc" Pierce whose family started the Williamsburg restaurant. The dining area is fairly plain, still reminiscent of a diner from decades ago. The service

is very fast so you can usually get food to go in a matter of several minutes unless there's a long line. You order at the counter, get a number, and then pick up your food when your number is called. Sides include Southern favorites like collard greens, cornbread, potato salad, hushpuppies, and even sweet potato "stix." You can also take home Pierce's original or honey barbecue sauces by the jar, or purchase a barbecue sauce gift basket. The restaurant sells other items like Pierce's roasted barbecue peanuts by the tin and souvenir mugs too. It's open 10:00 a.m. to 9:00 p.m. daily, except on Thanksgiving, Christmas and New Year's. (*$*)

RED CITY BUFFET

(3044 Richmond Rd. Unit 7 ☎ 757.221.0888

📱 **redcitybuffet.com)** This casual restaurant is located at Patriot Plaza. It offers an all-you-can-eat buffet with a combination of Japanese and Chinese cuisine. Choose from the usual Asian foods like General Tso's chicken, fried dumplings, and wonton soup, or sushi, soup, or a salad. The food includes lots of seafood on the buffet, ranging from spicy cuttlefish to scallop stuffed clam and baked salmon. The buffet also dishes out a few desserts. (*$$*)

SONIC DRIVE-IN

(721 E. Rochambeau Dr. ☎ 757.258.9100 📱 sonicdrivein.com) Sonic can be a lifesaver when you're hungry for a quick snack or meal, but just don't feel like getting out of the car. Diners can park the car and order to have a car hop bring the food out. There's also a drive-through for those who just want to grab something quickly and go. The limeades are delicious and a change of pace from sodas. They come in regular or diet and a variety of flavors. (*$*)

SWEET MADELINE'S CAFÉ & CATERING

(4680 Monticello Ave. Suite 16-B ☎ 757.220.3131) This quaint café serves delicious, gourmet sandwiches, soups, salads, and desserts, all homemade. Diners can eat in the café or get a boxed lunch to go. The sandwiches here have an out-of-the-ordinary flavor. Try the Monte Cristo with ham, turkey, and cheeses served with raspberry mayo on Texas toast sprinkled with sugar for around $9. This includes a side item, like the café's own Southern Salad, a unique combination of peas, carrots, country ham, red-roasted peppers, cheeses, and dressing. The portabella panini is also very popular here, as is the country chicken salad with raisins, apples, and walnuts. The café currently serves lunch only, but is starting to occasionally offer dinner so check ahead. Open daily except Sundays and major holidays.

TASTE TEA SALON AND GIFTS

(1915 Pocahontas Trail ☎ 757.221.9550 🖰 tasteteasalon.com) Have a full afternoon tea at this combination tea room and gift shop at the **Village Shops** at **Kingsmill**, run by Diana Dean, her sister Cherri Fiorenza, and mother Lillian Croft. Tea begins with scones baked daily, followed by a petite soup, and then a tiered tray with a variety of tea sandwiches, savories, and desserts. The shop sells Arney & Sons Tea by the tin or loose by the ounce, as well as a nice mix of gifts including teapots, cups and saucers, candles, home décor, handbags, lotions, fragrances, children's toys, and nursery items. Seating is limited at this small shop so reservations are required for tea. Closed Sunday and Monday.

THE POLO CLUB RESTAURANT & TAVERN

(1303 Jamestown Rd. ☎ 757.220.1122 🖰 poloclubrestaurant.com) The service is great in this friendly, family-owned restaurant established in 1989. It's known for its fantastic burgers cooked to order. There are many to choose from. The Poloburger is topped with sautéed onions, mushrooms, bacon, chili, and three cheeses. The menu also offers all kinds of sandwiches, homemade quiches, soups and salads. There are plenty of entrées to pick from too, ranging from pan fried pork chops to grilled teriyaki salmon. There's a full bar with a small selection of wines. The atmosphere is typical of a tavern, a little bit rustic and very casual. The restaurant is located in Colony Square Shopping Center and is open daily. *($$)*

WASABI ORIENTAL BUFFET

(1203 Richmond Rd. ☎ 757.345.6617 🔋 wasabiwmbg.com)

Better than your typical Asian buffet, the large all-you-can-eat spread at this casual, friendly restaurant offers options for just about anyone. The buffet has Mongolian and sushi bars, plus special fare for vegetarians, and seafood like steamed mussels and baby clams. For something unusual, sample the octopus salad, or go with traditional fare like Thai chicken or garlic eggplant, all worth tasting. The seaweed salad and the sesame balls stuffed with red bean paste are also good. Add crab legs to your plate for a few dollars extra. They have a small selection of wines, and imported and domestic beers to complement your meal. The restaurant is open every day for lunch and dinner. *($$)*

NIGHTLIFE AND BARS

Williamsburg offers as much entertainment by night as it does by day. Listed below are some recommended spots to unwind with a glass of wine or mug of beer following a full day's sightseeing.

BUFFALO WILD WINGS GRILL AND BAR

(4918 Courthouse St. ☎ 757.229.6099 🖱 buffalowildwings.com)
This fairly new restaurant in the Buffalo Wild Wings chain
is located in New Town. It's a great place to hang out with
friends or to catch a football or basketball game. You'll find
spicy chicken wings and all the typical foods, ranging from ribs
to salads. The restaurant is large and has lots of televisions
showing various sports competitions. There's a full bar and 25
beers on tap. Open late. *($)*

THE CORNER POCKET

(4805 Courthouse St. ☎ 757.220.0808 🖱 thecornerpocket.us)
This upscale restaurant and bar has an outdoor patio and a
large separate billiards room. The establishment serves lunch,
dinner and appetizers, with its full menu served until midnight.
They offer live music featuring national blues and zydeco acts.
The restaurant also hosts weekly pool tournaments and is open
daily. There is free Wi-Fi available here. *($$)*

GAMBOLS

(109 East Duke of Gloucester St. ☎ 757.229.2141
🖱 **colonialwilliamsburgresort.com/dining/chownings)** Located
in **Chowning's Tavern** in Colonial Williamsburg's Historic
Area, Gambols is a nightly entertainment program for before
or after dinner. Costumed balladeers lead diners in sing-alongs
and colonial games while they snack on peanuts and light food
items. Drinks offered include wines and ales, as well as ginger
ale and draft root beer. Entertainment earlier in the evening
is for families, but after 8:00 p.m., the program caters to adult
audiences. No reservations are needed. *($$)*

GREEN LEAFE

(765 Scotland St. ☎ 757.220.3405; 4345 New Town Ave. ☎ 757.221.9582 ♠ greenleafe.com) This popular local tavern offers good food and good times. With over 60 drafts on tap and 150 brands of bottled beer, it claims to have the best beer selection in southeastern Virginia. It was also named a top ten bar by *USA Today*. Its downtown location is just across the street from the **College of William and Mary's** football stadium, so it's a popular hangout for students as well as locals. Its second restaurant recently opened at New Town. Both locations offer live music, karaoke, and special parties throughout the year. Breakfast, lunch, and dinner are served at both places. Diners can choose from all types of burgers, pizza, sandwiches, wraps, and salads. For a more traditional meal, they can try pan-seared crab cakes, baby back ribs, and other platters. These come in two convenient sizes: "keg" for those with hearty appetites and a smaller "sixtel" portion for those not wanting as much to eat. There's a separate menu for children with items like pasta, grilled cheese, pizza, and chicken tenders for around $5. Both restaurants are open daily 365 days a year. *($)*

J. M. RANDALL'S CLASSIC AMERICAN GRILL AND TAVERN

(4854 Longhill Rd. ☎ 757.259.0406 ♠ jmrandalls.com) This is a nice place to wind down and listen to live jazz and blues music while enjoying a drink or a meal. There's live entertainment most nights of the week, and on other nights there are activities like karaoke, poker tournaments, or sports-themed activities. The menu has a New Orleans' flair, with entrées like Bourbon Kist Ribeye and Down in the Bayou with Andouille sausage, crawfish, and oysters served on penne pasta with Cajun cream sauce. *($$)*

Restaurants
in the Area

PITCHER'S

(50 Kingsmill Rd. ☎ 757.220.2500) Located in the **Williamsburg Marriott,** this sports bar and lounge has a pub-style menu. For sports fans there are over 20 satellite televisions, plus darts, pool tables, trivia games, and more. Pitcher's is open daily for lunch and dinner. *($$)*

TRENDY, UPSCALE, AND FINE DINING

The restaurants in this section offer a bit more upscale fine dining, for a more sophisticated culinary experience.

ABERDEEN BARN

(1601 Richmond Rd. ☎ 757.229.6661 ⬤ aberdeen-barn.com) This steakhouse serves quality food from its open hearth grill in a formal yet relaxed atmosphere. It's well known in the Williamsburg area for its fine steaks and prime rib. Other dishes include lamb, chicken, and a variety of seafood appetizers, soups, and entrées. Diners can have oysters on the half shell to start out, followed by a bowl of creamy shrimp and scallop bisque, and then an entrée like the Seafood Trilogy. This dish has scallops, jumbo shrimp, and salmon baked in champagne-mushroom sauce. All entrées are served with a fresh garden salad and potato choice or rice. Several dessert wines are offered to diners to accompany mouth-watering desserts like Bourbon Kentucky Pecan Pie and Five Layer 24k Carrot Cake. There's also a lounge serving a large selection of wines, beers, after-dinner drinks, "bartinis," and specialty coffees (alcoholic). The Aberdeen Barn opens daily at 5:00 p.m. and serves only dinner. *($$$)*

BONEFISH GRILL

(5212 Monticello Ave. ☎ 757.229.3474 🖰 bonefishgrill.com)

This fairly new upscale restaurant is located at New Town. The chain features fresh grilled fish and seafood served with a variety of sauces like warm mango salsa and lemon butter. Choose from a large variety of fish ranging from rainbow trout to Atlantic swordfish, as well as other seafood like lobster and scallops. The restaurant also has a few pork, chicken, and beef entrées, including steaks. The soups, salads, and appetizers are all delicious. The wine list is decent and a nice selection of martinis and cocktails is also offered from the full bar. Children's menus are available. The restaurant stays open daily. *($$)*

CAPTAIN GEORGE'S SEAFOOD RESTAURANT

(5363 Richmond Rd. ☎ 757.565.2323 🖰 captaingeorges.com)

This is the place for diners who love seafood and can't get enough of it. The restaurant offers a huge all-you-can-eat buffet packed with seafood favorites. Diners are likely to find their favorite seafood dish here as the selection is large. Choose from Alaskan snow crab legs, fried oysters, and softshell crabs, steamed mussels and shrimp, stuffed clams, broiled salmon, Mahi Mahi, and so much more. There are also a few non-seafood entrées on the buffet like prime rib, broiled and fried chicken, manicotti, and barbecued ribs. The buffet also has salad and soups like New England clam chowder and she crab. Sides include corn-on-the-cob, rice, baby potatoes, and other traditional fare. Dessert items range from baklava and flan, to cobblers and strawberry shortcake. The buffet is priced just under $30 for adults, is at half price for children between 5 and 12 years of age, and is free to children 4 and under. The early-bird special on Sunday is a little less expensive. If someone is not up for the buffet, the restaurant does offer a small à la carte menu and a separate children's menu. There's also a lounge and a full bar. This restaurant is not one-of-a-kind, but there are only five locations, three in Virginia, one on North Carolina's Outer Banks and one in Myrtle Beach. Open for dinner daily except Christmas Day. They open early on Sundays at noon. *($$$)*

CARRABBA'S ITALIAN GRILL

(2500 Richmond Rd. ☎ 757.564.3696 ⬤ carrabbas.com) This Italian restaurant franchise serves brick-oven pizzas, a large selection of pasta dishes, and items cooked on its wood-burning grill. These include seafood, steaks, and chicken. Try the Pollo Rosa Maria, chicken stuffed with fontina cheese and prosciutto, topped with mushrooms and basil lemon butter sauce for around $15. Classic dishes like lasagna and chicken parmesan are served with a house salad or soup. They have a decent selection of wines. The atmosphere is casual and inviting, and there's a special "Bambini" menu for little ones. There is also full bar and a separate bar menu. The restaurant stays open every day. *($$)*

CITIES GRILLE AND WINE SHOP

(4511-C John Tyler Hwy. ☎ 757.564.0269 ⬤ citiesgrille.com) This restaurant has about 150 wines diners can choose from to complement their meal, or they can purchase a bottle to take home. The atmosphere is upscale yet comfortable, with a large open dining area. The lunch menu offers five types of sliders and a half-pound Kobe beef burger with cheese or smoked bacon, sandwiches, soups, and salads. For dinner, entrées range from a grilled flat-iron steak to peach pecan catfish. Some of the dishes are complex, like the Camden Yard Bird, Baltimore, made of gulf shrimp sautéed with country ham, onions, mushrooms, and tomatoes in wine sauce tossed in pasta with chicken. The restaurant features a full bar and is open daily. *($$)*

DUDLEY'S FARMHOUSE GRILLE

(7816 Richmond Rd., Toano ☎ 757.566.1157

⛿ **dudleysfarmhousegrille.com)** Enjoy a really delicious meal in this 1905 country farmhouse. Besides beef, lamb, and seafood, you'll find an interesting selection of wild game on the menu. If you are game, try the wild boar with blackberry and port wine sauce, or pan-seared twin quail breast with mustard, cream, white wine, and chive sauce. Choose from over 100 wines. Open Tuesdays through Sundays. *($$)*

FOOD FOR THOUGHT

(1647 Richmond Rd. ☎ 757.645.4665

⛿ **foodforthoughtrestaurant.com)** This restaurant honors great minds and encourages its guests to think. Their themed menu offers items like Da Vinci Dippers, an appetizer with cheese-filled ravioli crusted with Italian bread crumbs and parmesan cheese served with marinara. Dinner entrées include old-fashioned favorites like Grandma's Meatloaf and Fork Tender Pot Roast, as well as contemporary dishes. They serve great sandwiches ranging from shrimp po' boys to a jerk chicken salad croissant. Open daily for lunch and dinner. *($$)*

ICHIBAN

(4905 Courthouse St. ☎ 757.253.8898 ⛿ ichibannewtown.com) This local favorite has the reputation of having the best sushi in town. Chinese and Thai cuisine, soups, and salads are also served in their charming dining room. *($$)*

LE YACA RESTAURANT FRANCAIS

(1915 Pocahontas Trail, Suite C-10 ☎ 757.220.3616

⬤ leyacawilliamsburg.com) Authentic French cuisine is offered at this fine restaurant located in the **Village Shops at Kingsmill.** It is owned by Chef Daniel Abid. The atmosphere in the main dining room is simple and elegant. One area is open and airy with lots of windows and the other is more private with low lighting. The areas are divided by a huge bold fireplace with a cooking hearth and a bar. Diners have the option of trying a variety of items from the à la carte menu. Items on the menu vary from appetizers like pan-seared duck liver with caramelized white peach and port wine sauce, to classic entrées like a roasted rack of lamb. Diners can choose from options on the three-course lunch and dinners menus as well. There's also a five-course meal offered for dinner for around $50. They have a small selection of beer and a large selection of American and French wines. Reservations are recommended. Open daily for lunch and dinner. *($$$)*

MAURIZIO'S ITALIAN RESTAURANT

(264-E McLaws Circle ☎ 757.229.0337

⬤ mauriziositalianrestaurant.com) This is a gourmet Italian restaurant with a classy, slightly upscale environment. It is located in the **Festival Market Place** shopping center off Route 60 near **Busch Gardens.** It's run by Sicilian-born chef and owner Maurizio Fiorello and his family. The food here is great, as are the addictive garlic bread knots served with the meal. There is much to choose from on the menu including vegetarian choices like the Eggplant Cacciatore and Gnocchi with Spinach, or pasta dishes such as Linguini Carbonara and Penne La Girgliata. The restaurant serves numerous chicken, veal, and seafood entrées. Try the scallops and tiger shrimp in a pink vodka sauce. They also serve traditional and European-style pizzas, calzones, Stromboli, salads, and a variety of appetizers. Children have their own menu with choices like personal cheese or pepperoni pizzas and chicken tenders with fries. Maurizio's has a nice selection of wine and a full bar. *($$)*

NAWAB INDIAN CUISINE

(204 Monticello Ave. ☎ 757.565.3200 🍴 nawabonline.com) This restaurant, with three other locations in the Tidewater area, is popular and has a good reputation for its excellent North Indian cuisine. The white table cloths and simple décor give the dining area an elegant feel. The prices are also reasonable for the quality of the food, which is prepared fresh daily without preservatives. A selection of breads baked in the clay oven fired with natural wood charcoal is served here. Entrées include a variety of meats, including seafood, poultry, beef, lamb, and goat. If you cannot decide what to have, try the Mixed Grill featuring individually marinated and roasted chicken, lamb, salmon, and shrimp. There are vegetarian options, as well as some vegan. Wine is offered either by the glass or bottle. Open daily for lunch and dinner. *($$)*

SECOND STREET

(140 Second St. ☎ 757.220.2286 🍴 secondst.com) This cozy restaurant with its dark wood and large beams has a tavern feel and bistro-style menu. It's located a few minutes from Colonial Williamsburg and is most popular for its burgers. The menu includes chicken, pork, beef, and seafood, plus pasta dishes and flatbread pizzas. Dinner entrées include hand-cut beef and some seafood dishes like caramelized sea scallops and 2nd Street Shrimp and Grits. If you want to taste something different, try the Grilled Colorado Bison Meatloaf. Drinks

Restaurants in the Area **123**

include an extensive wine menu and an interesting mix of martinis and cocktails, plus several draft beers and more in the bottle. Open daily for lunch and dinner, plus brunch on Sundays, with slightly reduced hours in the winter so check ahead. *($$)*

SHACKLEFORD'S II

(4640 Monticello Ave. #7 ☎ 757.258.5559 🖱 shacklefords.com) Located in Monticello Marketplace, this restaurant serves delicious seafood items including a delectable crab cake. There's a raw bar and a variety of seafood appetizers and steamed pots. If you're really hungry, try the Big Daddy Steamer with oysters, clams, a half-pound of shrimp and a half-pound of snow crab legs for around $30. They also serve steaks, some chicken dishes, and a good selection of hot sandwiches and salads. Desserts range from key lime pie to crème brulee and are priced reasonably. There is an extensive wine list as well as a large selection of liquers, cognacs, scotches and coffee drinks. There's a children's menu too. It is open daily for lunch and dinner and serves brunch on Sundays. *($$)*

VICTORIA'S RESTAURANT

(5269 John Tyler Hwy. ☎ 757.253.2233 🖱 victoriaswilliamsburg.com) Located in the **Williamsburg Crossing Shopping Center**, this casual restaurant is popular for its fine American food. It serves breakfast, lunch, and dinner. The large breakfast menu includes omelets, pancakes, bagels, eggs cooked to order, and lots of popular Southern sides like grits, stewed apples, biscuits and gravy, plus much more. You can have a mimosa or Bloody Mary with your Eggs Benedict as well. For lunch, the restaurant offers a large selection of salads, hero sandwiches, burgers, and entrées like crab cakes with fries and slaw. It also offers she crab soup and tomato bisque, plus a soup of the day. For dinner, the restaurant features additional seafood, steak, and pasta selections. There's also a children's menu. Dine on the outdoor brick patio if the weather is nice. The restaurant has a full bar. Open daily except Tuesdays. *($$)*

THE WHITEHALL RESTAURANT
(1325 Jamestown Rd. ☎ 757.229.4663 ☙ thewhitehall.com)
European-style dining is offered in a formal dining room setting at this restaurant located in an historic 19th-century building. The menu includes traditional dishes like lamb chops, Angus sirloin steak, veal scallopine and fresh Atlantic salmon. Vegetarians can feast on a selection of salads, pasta, and "Melanzane"-eggplant stuffed with rice, onions, mushrooms, roasted peppers, ricotta cheese served on a bed of pine nuts, currants, and sautéed spinach. The **King's Lounge and Terrace** has a nice selection of cocktails and martinis, with a separate menu offering beer battered shrimp, calamari, steak and chips, and more. Open only for dinner Thursdays through Saturdays. *($$$)*

A walk through President's Park

Captain John Smith overlooks the James River at Historic Jamestowne

Colonial figures sold at the Colonial Williamsburg Visitor Center

Memorial Church at Historic Jamestowne

The Colonial Capitol

Watermen's Museum at Yorktown

Places to Stay in the Williamsburg Area

In addition to the Colonial Williamsburg lodging options, there are literally hundreds of accommodations in the Williamsburg area. Accommodations included here are just a sample of the places available in Williamsburg. One of our favorite hotels is the **Great Wolf Lodge Resort**, which has an indoor water park.

Standard room rate in peak season starts at under $100 = ($), $100-$200 = ($$), and above $200 = ($$$).

HOTELS

Among the plethora of different kinds of accommodations available in Williamsburg, there are several good hotels where visitors can choose to stay.

AMERICA'S BEST VALUE INN
(119 Bypass Rd. ☎ 800.283.1663 🖱 americasbestvalueinn.com)
This budget hotel is in a good central location making it easy to get to all Williamsburg attractions and outlet shops. It's also adjacent to several restaurants including **Cracker Barrel** and **Golden Corral**. It offers a complimentary breakfast with Belgian waffles, hard-boiled eggs, biscuits, fruits, cereals, and more. Rooms feature pillow-top beds, irons and ironing boards, hair dryers, premium cable television, and high-speed Internet access. The hotel is rated *AAA Two Diamond*. It has an outdoor pool and is pet-friendly. *($)*

CROWNE PLAZA WILLIAMSBURG HOTEL AT FORT MAGRUDER

(6945 Pocahontas Trail ☎ 757.220.2250
🖱 cpwilliamsburghotel.com) This hotel is located within a few minutes of Colonial Williamsburg. It has both rooms and suites with sitting rooms and wet bars. All rooms are well equipped and include refrigerators, large televisions with premium cable, irons and ironing boards, and hair dryers. Most rooms have either a patio or balcony. There are two dining establishments on-site, the **Veranda Dining Room Restaurant** and **J.B.'s Tavern**, a casual sports bar and 24-hour lounge. There is also a hot tub, game room, fitness center, tennis courts, and indoor and outdoor pools. This hotel is both pet- and earth-friendly. *($$)*

COUNTRY HEARTH INN AND SUITES WILLIAMSBURG

(924 Capitol Landing Rd. ☎ 757.229.5215 🖱 countryhearth.com)
This hotel has a homey feel and the rooms feature country décor. Amenities include an outdoor pool and complimentary breakfast. Rooms have satellite television, hair dryers, and free high-speed Internet. No pets are allowed. *($)*

DAYS INN WILLIAMSBURG CENTRAL

(1900 Richmond Rd. ☎ 757.229.6600
🖱 daysinn.com/hotel/15504) This *AAA Two Diamond* hotel is located within a few minutes' drive of the **Prime Outlets, Williamsburg Pottery**, and the **Williamsburg Outlet Mall**. It is right next to **Red Lobster** and **Olive Garden** restaurants. Rooms are clean, but not very large and the bathrooms are also fairly small. Rooms include cable television with HBO, microwaves, refrigerators, irons, and ironing boards. A free compli-

mentary breakfast is served in the breakfast room. There's an outdoor pool. No pets are permitted. *($)*

EMBASSY SUITES WILLIAMSBURG

(3006 Mooretown Rd. ☎ 757.229.6800

🖱 embassysuites1.hilton.com) This centrally located hotel has a lovely atrium-style lobby with plants, a flowing fountain, and lots of seating. Rooms are modern and clean. Bedrooms are not overly large, but suites also have living areas with sofa beds, a dining/work area, and kitchenettes with microwaves and refrigerators. They also include a video-game console, satellite television, and free high-speed Internet access. There's an indoor pool with modern design, a well-equipped fitness center, and a restaurant which serves a complimentary cooked-to-order breakfast (open for breakfast only). The casual **Atrium Café and Lounge** serves American cuisine nightly. Smoking is allowed in designated areas only. The hotel does not allow pets. *($$)*

GREAT WOLF LODGE

(549 East Rochambeau Dr. ☎ 757.229.9700/800.551.9653

🖱 greatwolf.com/williamsburg/waterpark) This family-friendly resort hotel features a huge indoor 67,000-square-foot water park with giant slides, a wave pool, and a towering treehouse waterfront that is four-stories tall. It allows families and kids to splash around in its water park throughout the year. There's also an outdoor pool, arcade, luxurious full-service spa, multiple restaurants, and a bar. Suites have a camping-lodge theme, and feature various sleeping configurations. The Wolf Den Suite comes with a separate sleeping "den" for children. In the cozy hut-like area, a child has a fun semi-private "room" with a bunk bed and plasma television. There are many other configurations with additional themes and rooms. The resort has over 400 suites which come with mini-refrigerators, microwaves, hair dryers, and a wet bar. No smoking or pets allowed. *($$$)*

HILTON GARDEN INN

(1624 Richmond Rd. ☎ 757.253.9400

⬤ williamsburg.gardeninn.com) This *AAA Three Diamond* hotel is in a central location in between Colonial Williamsburg and all the outlet shops. Rooms are spacious and have refrigerators, microwaves, large comfortable arm chairs, ergonomically-designed desks and chairs, two phones, hair dryers, free high-speed Internet, and cable television. Guests can also choose suites with living room areas. There's a pool, whirlpool, fitness center, 24-hour convenience mart, restaurant, and lounge on-site. No pets are allowed here. *($$)*

HOLIDAY INN-EXPRESS HOTEL AND SUITES

(1452 Richmond Rd. ☎ 757.941.1057 ⬤ hiexpress.com) This hotel includes modern clean rooms and suites. They come with hair dryers, microwaves, mini refrigerators, irons and ironing boards, satellite television, and high-speed Internet access. There's an indoor pool, gift shop, and a small fitness center. A free deluxe complimentary breakfast is offered in a large open dining area. This hotel does not allow pets. *($$)*

HOWARD JOHNSON

(6483 Richmond Rd. ☎ 757.220.5550

⬤ the.hojo.com/Williamsburg/11801) This hotel is only a few minutes from the **Williamsburg Pottery, Williamsburg Outlet Mall**, and **Prime Outlets**. It is a fairly inexpensive place to stay for those on a budget, with a restaurant and cocktail bar on-site. There is also a large indoor swimming pool and an exercise room with a sauna. All guest rooms have refrigerators and microwaves and some rooms also have Jacuzzis. Guests are treated to a complimentary continental breakfast in the mornings. Non-smoking rooms are available. No pets allowed here. *($)*

MOTELS

If you want to save a few bucks on lodging, these motels offer good, clean accommodation at more affordable rates.

MOTEL ROCHAMBEAU
(929 Capitol Landing Rd. ☎ 757.229.2851

🖰 motelrochambeau.com) This quaint motel is within a short drive of Colonial Williamsburg and the theme parks. It's been a family-run motel for two generations now operated by David and Michelle Bryhn. Rooms are simple and clean, featuring free wireless Internet and cable television. There's free coffee and a public-access computer in the lobby. There are also grilling and picnic areas with access to the pool at the **White Lion**. This pet-friendly motel is seasonal and closes for the winter months. *($)*

WHITE LION MOTEL
(912 Capitol Landing Rd. ☎ 757.229.2708

🖰 whitelionmotel.com) This older motel is within a short drive of Colonial Williamsburg, **Busch Gardens**, and **Water Country USA**. It's not fancy, but it is an economical place to stay especially if you have a large family. The motel's efficiency and two-bedroom suites accommodate up to seven persons. Its adorable colonial cottages, which are its basic rooms, sleep four persons. Pets are allowed here. *($)*

CAMPGROUNDS

For tourists interested in experiencing nature and the great outdoors, these campsites equipped with necessary amenities are
good options for a few nights' or week-long stay.

ANVIL CAMPGROUND

**(5243 Mooretown Rd. ☎ 757.565.2300
🖱 anvilcampground.com)** This family-operated campground
offers camping sites for tents and RVs and also has two
cottages. A Williamsburg Transport Service shuttle bus stops
here, giving campers the convenience of leaving the driving
to someone else for a minimal charge. Amenities include a
laundry room, game room, pool, playgrounds, and free high-
speed Internet access. There are also some simple nice touches
like free coffee all day and a public-access computer. Each
camping site has a picnic table and fire ring, and premium sites
offer cable television. There's a camp store and gift shop. This
campground remains open year-round.

WILLIAMSBURG KOA KAMPGROUND

(4000 Newman Rd. ☎ 757.565.2734 🖱 williamsburgkoa.com)
This resort-style campground offers 40 cabins, as well as pull-
through sites for RVs and tent sites. Campers will find amenities like cable television, free Wi-Fi service, and a 24-hour
laundry. There are also grocery stores, gift shops, nature trails,
game rooms, and two heated pools. There are play areas for
children, as well as special programs in the summer. Cabins can
sleep only four persons and no pets are allowed in them. The
cabins do not have bathrooms, but shared facilities are close
by. Bring your own bedding, linens, and cooking and eating
utensils. Open March through December.

Shopping in the Area

Williamsburg is one of the largest outlet shopping destinations in America. Most of the outlet shops are concentrated near the Lightfoot area, about a ten-minute drive from the Historic Area. **Prime Outlets** with over a hundred name-brand stores is one of the top ten outlet malls in the country.

The well-known **Williamsburg Pottery** is also located in this area. Though it seems to have lost some of its luster in recent years as newer trendier shops have moved into town, it still has one of the largest inventories in the area and is a fantastic place to find a bargain or a unique gift. Recent renovations make it easier for customers to find what they're looking for as well.

Yankee Candle is a huge new shop that is more like a village. It even snows there every day. It sells loads of candles and a whole lot more. The nearby **Williamsburg Outlet Mall** is the area's only indoor mall. It has around 30 stores selling brands like Totes, Lee, and Wrangler.

This chapter has two sections. The first describes some of the shopping places that have multiple stores like shopping centers and malls, as well as some of the larger stores. The second lists a few of the many unique shops you'll find in the area.

SHOPPING MALLS, CENTERS, AND LARGER STORES

If you feel at home in the midst of well-known brands and labels at large shopping complexes, Williamsburg has more than its fair share of choices.

COLONY SQUARE SHOPPING CENTER

(1200-1300 Jamestown Rd.) This shopping center off Jamestown Road has a nice coffeeshop, a used book store, a pleasant restaurant called **The Polo Club Restaurant & Tavern**, a food market, and two interesting gift shops, **Morrison's Flowers & Gifts and Kinks, Quirks & Caffeine**. There is also a jewelry store here. Around the holidays, the center holds an open house with special sales and activities.

MARQUIS TOWNE CENTER

(I-199 adjacent to Water Country USA near I-604) This new shopping center is located adjacent to **Water Country USA**, and is near **Busch Gardens** and **President's Park**. It is somewhat out of the way unless you are visiting one of these parks or traveling to Yorktown. So far it only has five large new anchor stores. They are Best Buy, Kohl's, Dick's Sporting Goods, JC Penney, and Target.

NEW TOWN

(4801 Courthouse St. 🖱 newtownwilliamsburg.com) A new urban mixed-use village still being developed, this is the trendiest new place to shop and dine in Williamsburg. It features many of the shops you also find in area malls such as PacSun, Victoria's Secret, and Footlocker. There are upscale shops like Ann Taylor Loft and specialty stores like Lane Bryant. Some one-of-a-kind shops can be found here too. At the **Nautical Dog**, you can find a new outfit or treat for your four-legged friends, or shop for the two-legged variety at **Paisley** (🖱 *paisleygifts.com*), a shop selling whimsical and seasonal gifts and home décor. There's a huge selection of restaurants to choose from, whether you want to grab a sub sandwich or are planning an elegant dinner for two. They range from trendy chains like

Bonefish Grill to unique one-of-kinds like **artcafe26**, a combination art gallery and modern European-style café. **Ichiban**, one of Williamsburg's best sushi bars, is located here as well. See the Restaurants in the Area chapter for more information.

PRIME OUTLETS

(5715-62a Richmond Rd. ☎ 757.565.0702 🖰 primeoutlets.com)
Shoppers will find a huge assortment of items with top-brand names at this large outdoor shopping mall with 120 stores and a small food court. This center is sprawling with shops fairly spread out over a large area. The shops wrap around vast parking areas and the place is so large that you may prefer to drive from some shops to others. However, you can certainly walk to those close by. This mall is very popular so the traffic can be heavy getting in and out of the entrances on weekends or around the holidays.

The mall has shops which sell men's and women's clothing, and include brands like Brooks Brothers, Eddie Bauer, Juicy Couture, Nautica, Michael Kors, Kenneth Cole, Tommy Hilfiger, Van Heusen, GUESS, Haggar, Coldwater Creek, and dozens of others.

It's also a great place to get name-brand shoes cheaper than at the department stores, although they are still not always inexpensive as some were very expensive to begin with. Shoppers here will find names like Vans, ALDO, Stride Rite, Nike, Naturalizer, Nine West, and others. There are specialty stores as well like Bath & Body Works, Harry & David, Maidenform, and Jockey. If you like handbags, there's a Dooney & Bourke and Coach. There are also close to ten jewelry stores, over a half-dozen home fashion stores, and around a dozen stores selling children's apparel.

Open daily, except for Easter, Thanksgiving, and Christmas Day.

THE VILLAGE SHOPS AT KINGSMILL

(1915 Pocahontas Trail) It's a pleasure to walk around this outdoor shopping center near **Busch Gardens**. As you stroll down its long walkways, you feel like you're walking through a quaint village. There's a wide range in the products that the shops offer. On one side of the center, there is a Harley Davidson store and on the other there is a specialty wine and cheese shop. There's an upscale consignment shop, a knitting and quilting shop, a fine jewelry store, and more. Some of the spaces here are not retail shops but house offices instead. There are several places to eat ranging from an elegant French restaurant to a small tea salon.

WILLIAMSBURG ANTIQUE MALL

(500 Lightfoot Rd. ☎ 757.565.3422 🖱 antiqueswilliamsburg.com) This huge 45,000-square foot mall sells all sorts of antique, vintage, and collectible items offered by more than 300 vendors. The mall is very well laid out and items are well labeled with descriptions as well as prices. Some pieces are locked behind glass, but many others are not. There's something here for almost every collector, from Pez dispensers and vintage thermoses to oyster plates and coins. You'll also find a large selection of books, carved duck decoys, Lionel trains, pottery and glass, ivory figurines, toys, kitchen items, paintings, jewelry, and steel and wood engravings, some from the Civil War. This is just the tip of the iceberg, so to speak. Plan to spend some time browsing around here. Most items are priced to value, but there are some good bargains as well. Pricing varies from vendor to vendor. The tiny but elegantly decorated **Petite Tea Room** at the mall serves soups, sandwiches, home-made sweets, and a variety of teas and other beverages. The mall is open daily except Easter, Thanksgiving, and Christmas Day.

WILLIAMSBURG CROSSING SHOPPING CENTER

(5200 John Tyler Hwy.) This shopping center has a Bloom supermarket, a coffee shop, several hair salons, and quite a few places to eat. There are a number of fast food outlets including Taco Bell, Subway, a Chinese takeout place, and Domino's and Papa John's takeout pizza shops. There is also a Mexican restaurant, a fine foods deli, and **Victoria's**, an award-winning restaurant serving American cuisine. If you need to mail any packages home, there is a UPS Store here as well.

YANKEE CANDLE WILLIAMSBURG ✪ Must See!

(2200 Richmond Rd. ☎ 877.616.6510 ♔ yankeecandle.com) Shoppers can choose from 400,000 candles here in 200 different Yankee Candle scents. This is a magical place to visit, whether you like candles or not. It is laid out like a village, with rooms giving the façade of shops in a town. They separate the larger store into specialty areas. Shoppers can stroll through the dimly lit Holiday Park alive with colorful Christmas trees and stars twinkling on the high ceiling. There is a "snow" fall here daily. The general store sells all kinds of kitchen items like bamboo cutting boards, and gadgets ranging from avocado slicers to tuna presses. It sells foods like salsas, syrups, preserves and honey, and collectible figurines in brands like The Trail of Painted Ponies and Cow Parade. The Home Store sells home décor and garden items. Find everything here from garden flags and flower bulb kits to tea pots and dinnerware. Customers can buy fudge from another shop or visit **Popcornopolis** for a large selection of gourmet popcorn treats. There's also a candy store, a place to make your own dipped candles, and much more. Special events like artist's demonstrations and Santa visits are scheduled at various times. There's a small café to grab a bite to eat. Open daily except for Thanksgiving and Christmas.

LIGHTFOOT ANTIQUE MALL

(Richmond Rd. next to big Brass Shop in the Norge area) Not very impressive from outward appearances and not even on first walking inside, but this family-run business operated by the Jones's is larger than it seems at first. Plus there is some neat old thing waiting to be found in almost every nook and cranny. There are several side rooms and corridors and items offered from 40 separate vendors. If you like antiques and interesting old stuff, and don't mind doing a little searching to find treasure, prepare to spend some time here. Most items are quite reasonably priced. It stays open daily except on major holidays.

THE WILLIAMSBURG OUTLET MALL

(6401 Richmond Rd. ☎ 757.565.3378

☗ **williamsburgoutletmall.com)** Not far from the **Prime Outlets**, this one-story indoor mall has 250,000 feet of shopping space. It is Williamsburg's only enclosed outlet center. There are around 30 stores here selling men's and women's attire, shoes, vitamins, jewelry, and more. Find popular brands like Totes, Vanity Fair, Lee, Wrangler, and Black & Decker. There is a small store where you can buy your favorite Avon products and another shop selling Camelot Bears. Two shops here cater to sports fans, Team Sportswear and New Concept Gifts. There are many opportunities to find bargains and unusual items at this mall. The mall is not too large, and shoppers can shop here in any kind of weather without the hassle of getting in and out of the car. The mall has two places in its courtyard area to get a quick bite to eat or a drink, a Hershey's Malt Shoppe and Los Tres Gallos, which serves authentic Mexican food.

WILLIAMSBURG POTTERY ✪ Must See!
(6692 Richmond Rd. ☎ 757.564.3326

🖳 williamsburgpottery.com) Called simply "The Pottery" or "Pottery Factory" by many locals, this is a bargain shoppers' paradise. The number of shoppers seen here on any given day seems way down compared to a few years ago though when you could barely find a parking spot. The business has been making some changes though. At the time this book was being written, it was undergoing some changes and renovations. Some stores had closed and efforts were being made to move scattered items into more organized, theme-related shops.

The pottery needs a facelift now and then though, as it has been around for a long time. It humbly began more than 70 years ago when founder and potter James Maloney sold some dishes from his lawn along Route 60. He had bought a whole truckload of factory seconds, which sold like hotcakes for five cents apiece.

These days, tens of thousands of people reportedly shop here each year. The pottery is basically a large compound of warehouse-style buildings sprawled across a couple hundred acres, separated by a railroad track. It is still based on the site where Maloney made his first sale, and is still owned by his family.

The pottery's shops are more utilitarian than aesthetic though. The buildings are plain, lacking the general curb and sex appeal of the more upscale and higher-priced outlets which have opened nearby. Parts of the complex are downright ugly. But if you don't mind doing a bit of walking and rummaging through a large quantity of items inside, the pottery offers great potential for bargain hunters. There's also a good chance shoppers will find a thing or two here they've not found any place else.

Some items sold at the pottery are crafted on-site, including its salt-glazed ceramic pots. Floral arrangements and custom-designed lamps can be ordered by customers as well. There's also a frame shop with a huge selection of prints and posters to choose for framing. Thousands of plants for the pottery's garden center are also grown on site.

The solar building is still the largest shop at the complex housing Oriental, Christmas, wicker and frame shops, plus more. Another large building sells everything from gourmet specialty foods and wines to crystal stemware. The building adjacent to the greenhouse has been renovated into a linens store. It sells fine linens, bedding and home décor.

Several outlet stores at the mall are still located in the buildings closest to Richmond Road. These include a Pepperidge Farms store, a cigarette shop, and a store selling knives, swords, and leather goods.

The pottery is open daily year-round except on Christmas Day. When setting out for a full or partial day of shopping here, dress casually and wear comfortable shoes as you'll have the opportunity to do plenty of walking. If your shopping excursion whets your appetite, there is a cafeteria located at the pottery itself, which offers sandwiches and light fare.

As you make purchases, your items will be wrapped with newspaper and tape, the pottery's trademark form of packaging for decades. Cashiers will also tape your receipt to each package. A security guard checks your packages for receipts as you exit the gates so try not to lose them.

INTERESTING AND UNIQUE SHOPS

For a well-rounded shopping experience in Williamsburg, explore some of these extra-ordinary shops for one-of-a-kind souvenirs and gifts.

AMISH COUNTRY PRODUCTS
(7521 Richmond Rd. ☎ 800.786.0407

amishcountryproducts.com) Located in a small shopping center in the old Candle Factory at Norge, this shop sells handcrafted wooden furniture and home décor plus all types of food items from the Amish Country in Pennsylvania. These include breads, mixes, cheeses, snacks, nuts, spreads, candies, pickles, and more. Open Thursdays through Saturdays.

A TOUCH OF EARTH
(6580 Richmond Rd. ☎ 757.565.0425

atouchofearthgallery.com) This great shop is located at the Gallery Shops across the street from the **Williamsburg Outlet Mall**. It features the arts and handcrafts of close to 130 artists from all over the country, even from places as far away as California. It promotes works by many local artists as well. Potter Lianne Lurie and her husband, Paul Pittman, run the shop, which opened in 1977. Its main focus is still pottery, selling everything from urns to oven-safe cookware, to handmade plates, and coffee mugs. Shoppers will also find beautifully crafted wooden jewelry boxes, knitted and painted silk scarves, jewelry, metal and paper items, and much more. A Touch of Earth is open daily.

BASSETT'S CHRISTMAS SHOP

(207 Bypass Rd. ☎ 757.229.7648) This local one-of-a-kind store is smaller than some of the other year-round Christmas shops in the area, but its prices are very competitive. It also offers a good selection of items. The shop sells beautiful Porter music boxes, Bearington Bears, Webkinz, Madame Alexander dolls, and personalized ornaments and stockings. They also have items by Jim Shore, Dept. 56, Cat's Meow, Radko, and other brand names. The "12 Days of Christmas Charm Bracelet" is one of the affordable gifts sold at the shop, yours for around $12.

BERTRAM AND WILLIAMS BOOKS AND FINE ART
✪ Must See!

(1459 Richmond Rd. ☎ 757.564.9670 🖑 bertbook.com) This unassuming family-run gallery and shop is a must-see for art and book lovers alike. It houses over 25,000 used and rare books, plus a diverse collection of old maps, autographs, documents, and prints. Books range from contemporary non-fiction and fiction to books dating to the 16th century. You might not find today's pop sellers, but there is much to choose from among scholarly non-fiction and literary fiction. Prices are very affordable, with about half the shop's books selling for under $10. Framed art hangs on the walls between the bookshelves and unframed pieces can be easily browsed in large floor and table boxes. Choose from original lithographs, etchings, woodcuts, photographs, paintings, and antique prints. Shoppers will find an interesting range of artists and subjects, including an original lithograph by James McNeill Whistler of his brother called *The Doctor,* or a whimsical pastel drawing of George Burns wearing a grin and holding a cigar which includes his autograph. There are also pieces by popular artists of today like *Renaissance Man,* a colorful, richly textured original painting by Anna Carll. Book lovers can drop by anytime, as the bookstore remains open daily.

BOOK EXCHANGE OF WILLIAMSBURG

(1303 Jamestown Rd., Suite 106, Colony Square Shopping Center ☎ 757.220.3778) This bookstore sells lots of gently used books at reasonable prices. It's well organized and a good place to discover a good read and stays open daily.

CAMELOT BEARS ✪ Must See!

(6401 Richmond Rd. Suite 5 ☎ 757.565.9060
🖱 camelotbears.com) You can make your own bear at this fun and interesting shop located at the **Williamsburg Outlet Mall**. It has a King Arthur's theme and a mascot named Excalibear. Besides being able to make their own customized bears, shoppers will also find all sorts of plush bears by collectible brands like Steiff, Gund, Boyd's, Bearington, and others. There are also bear collectibles, jewelry, home décor, clothing, baby gifts, books, and more. The store provides educational information about the plight of bears in the wild, and donates a percentage of its Web sales to conservation efforts. Open daily.

CHRISTMAS MOUSE

(1991 Richmond Rd. ☎ 757.221.0357 🖱 christmasmouse.com)
Christmas is celebrated round the year at this store, which has locations in North and South Carolina, as well as the two locations in Williamsburg. The other is at 7461 Richmond

Road in the Norge area (☎ *757.229.8140)*. It's well worth the visit, whether you're doing some early holiday shopping or just want a little taste of the Christmas spirit in let's say, June or July. The shop features 50 beautifully decorated trees so it's a great place to stop by if nothing more than to get ideas. Find almost any kind of Christmas tree ornament imaginable in this two-story shop, and that's no exaggeration — there are 25,000 to choose from. They include refined pieces in brass, porcelain, and glass — the elegant mouth-blown Egyptian glass teapots engraved with 24-karat gold trim are beautiful. Then there are the pop culture pieces such as life-like miniature Elvis's, Betty Boops, and Southpark characters in resin, and animals of just about every species. There's an ornament for the lover of almost every sport and hobby, from fishing, hunting, golfing, NFL and college football, to shopping, cooking, and even gambling. There are sock monkeys knitted from yarn and "Just Married" stretch limos in plastic. You will also come across ornaments celebrating professions from lawyer to EMT, plus all the military branches. Again, it's hard to stress how many ornaments there are here, but shoppers will also find lots of artificial wreaths, stockings, Christmas village figures and cottages, angels, and all sorts of Santas, not just the traditional variety either. Here, Santas drink martinis, blow on bagpipes, cook pasta, and play games like soccer and chess. Nutcrackers also come in charming varieties — let the Wizard of Oz tin-man crack open your walnuts. Besides Christmas, there are limited items for other holidays like Halloween and a few pieces celebrating other cultures. Shoppers will find some items not specifically for the holidays too. These include wall plaques, wooden ship models, heirloom dolls, night lights, and more. Open daily except, ironically, Christmas Day!

CIVIL WAR AND NATIVE AMERICAN STORE AND GALLERY

(1441 Richmond Rd. ☎ 757.253.1155 📱 civilwar.nu) This is a great shop for history buffs, collectors, or anyone interested in the Civil War or Native American art and culture. You'll find handcrafted Native American pottery, jewelry, and dolls. Civil War items include limited edition prints by several artists, replica firearms, and swords, buckles, uniforms, flags, and more. There are also related items for children. The gallery remains open daily.

DOVETAIL ANTIQUES

(7521 Richmond Rd. ☎ 757.565.3553

📱 dovetailantiquesatnorge.com) This 3,600-square foot shop located at Norge near the Brass Shop has a varied selection of antiques neatly arranged and displayed so that it's easy to see and get to everything. They sell items ranging from large furniture pieces to antique clocks, books, paintings, and pottery. Most items are fairly priced and well labeled with details making it easy to identify what you are viewing. A sign on the door advises visitors to leave strollers and large bags in the car to avoid breaking anything. Shoppers can drop by here any day as the shop is open daily.

KINKS, QUIRKS & CAFFEINE

(1301 Jamestown Rd. ☎ 757.229.5889 📱 kinksandquirks.com) Whimsy is the word at this fun, eclectic shop. It is full of bright, colorful items from lime-green scarves with mini pom-poms to handmade jewelry and painted wine glasses. It features works by local artists and offers many one-of-a-kind items. There is also a small espresso counter in the back of the shop so shoppers can enjoy a warm beverage while looking around. The shop is open daily.

LOGOS BOOKSTORE & OUTLET

(6588 Richmond Rd. ☎ 757.564.6278) This store is located near Norge in the Gallery Shoppes. It sells a large selection of Christian books and other religious and inspirational items at both retail and outlet prices. Its bargain-priced greeting cards sell for around $1, and there are some bargain books under $5. Shoppers will find Bibles in various translations. There are Bibles for children, special ones for each branch of the military, and for careers. Bibles are available in Spanish and the shop also stocks *The Complete Jewish Bible*. Other items here include Bible covers and totes, choir robes, resources for pastors, and reference books like dictionaries, concordances, and atlases. Bibles are also offered on CD as are some other books. Choose from fiction or non-fiction books on topics like relationships, family, marriage, and finance. There are special selections for teens and children, plus some Bible-related games and toys.

MORRISON'S FLOWERS & GIFTS

(1303 Jamestown Rd., Suite 129 ☎ 757.220.1242) Much more than a full-service florist, this shop is beautifully decorated with many fine gifts, ranging from fine china to jewelry. There are many home décor items, candles, artwork, dried flower arrangements, and table centerpieces. Some jewelry and Baggallini handbags and wallets are also sold here.

OLD CHICKAHOMINY HOUSE

(1211 Jamestown Rd. ☎ 757.229.4689

oldchickahominyhouse.com) This is both a gift shop and restaurant set in a rustic plantation house setting. The gift shop has a nice selection of books on Virginia and the south in general. It also sells wine accessories, home décor, jewelry, some apparel, handbags, and seasonal holiday items. It is a nice choice of shop if you're looking to buy a card, stationery, or even an out-of-the-ordinary gift. The restaurant is popular for its Southern cooking, like Old Virginia ham biscuits and homemade pie. There is often a wait to be seated. Open daily except for Thanksgiving, Christmas, and July 4th. The store and restaurant both close two weeks in early January.

REVOLUTIONARY HARLEY-DAVIDSON

(1915 Pocahontas Trail, Unit F-5 ☎ 757.565.5122) This cool store located at the **Village Shops at Kingsmill** sells Harley-Davidson clothing, accessories, and collectibles.

SEASONS OF WILLIAMSBURG

(1308 Jamestown Rd. ☎ 757.565.4600

theseasonsofwilliamsburg.com) This pretty shop sells flowers, gifts, and accessories. Besides live flowers, it sells custom silk arrangements, home décor, and has a variety of gift items. There's also a nice selection of vintage and antique pieces including silver, glass, china, and linens. Open Monday through Saturday.

THE CANDY STORE OUTLET

(Rt. 60, Lightfoot ☎ 757.565.1151 ⬤ wythewill.com) This shop is great for those with a sweet tooth. There's a large selection of fudge and candies by the pound. You can also find other boxed and bar candies and snacks, nuts, and teas.

THE WILLIAMSBURG BRASS SHOP

(6967 Richmond Rd. ☎ 757.564.3395

⬤ williamsburgbrassshop.com) Located just west of the **Williamsburg Pottery**, this small shop sells brass figurines and other home décor items like candlesticks, door knockers, fireplace accessories, and a decent selection of both lamps and framed mirrors. Shoppers can find authentic colonial reproductions with brass, copper, iron and pewter finishes, plus many other pieces featuring animal and nautical themes. The shop also sells outdoor lighting fixtures, rim locks, switch plates, and Christmas ornaments by Baldwin. It can be visited anytime of the week as it is open daily.

THE WINE AND CHEESE SHOP AT KINGSMILL

(1915 Pocahontas Trail Suite D-6 ☎ 757.229.6754

⬤ potterywineandcheese.com) Located at the **Village Shops at Kingsmill**, this shop sells a large variety of international cheeses and wines from all over the world. There's an assortment of gift baskets to choose from, and gourmet food items ranging from chocolates and cookies to dips and salsas. Shoppers can also browse for gifts and kitchen items like utensils and glassware. This is a good place to find Virginia-made products. A deli serves sandwiches, homemade soups, and freshly baked cookies and desserts. There's a dining area and also an outdoor patio along the shopping plaza's walkway for dining when the weather is nice.

WALLACE'S TRADING POST

(1851 Richmond Rd. ☎ 757.564.6101

⬦ williamsburgsouvenirco.com) Find an interesting mix of souvenirs in this 10,000-square foot store, owned by the same company as the Williamsburg General Store, almost directly across the road. Prices are moderate, but not unreasonable. It's a good one-stop shop to find a souvenir for just about everyone in the family. There are lots of Williamsburg souvenirs to take back home, plus sports memorabilia, home décor, toys, Civil War and Native American items, and a selection of Minnetonka sandals and moccasins. A fudge factory sells homemade fudge here. Another interesting area of the store features a full-sized psychedelic VW Beetle, and is devoted to Peace Frogs' items like tee-shirts, key chains, bumper stickers, and more. There's even a video that shoppers can watch to learn more about that company's unique philanthropic ventures. The shop is open daily.

WILLIAMSBURG DOLL FACTORY

(7441 Richmond Rd. ☎ 757.564.9703 ⬦ dollfactory.com) This small boutique displays and sells large porcelain Lady Anne dolls by Margaret Anne Rothwell. Collectors often visit the shop to have their dolls signed by her and also to see dolls being made. The shop also sells dolls by Adora, Delton, Linda Rick, and Virginia Turner, plus some collectibles, and is open daily.

WILLIAMSBURG FINE ART

(6592 Richmond Rd. ☎ 757.564.9484

🖱 williamsburgfineart.com) Shoppers will not find any Giclees or prints here. This gallery and custom framing shop sells only quality, original art. Joseph Glosson, who owns the shop with his wife Eunice, is very friendly, unpretentious, and willing to spend time helping customers find the perfect piece. Paintings begin in the $100-dollar range for small oil paintings, and go up to several thousand dollars. Work is available from artists around the world including Heather Judge, Doris Pontieri, Linda Tullis, and Zini just to name a few. Once the right painting is chosen, the shop's master framer helps customers decide on the right molding to frame the piece. The shop sells 300 styles of molding, one of the largest selections offered on the East Coast. Open Mondays through Saturdays.

Enjoying The Great Outdoors

The area is rich with natural beauty so get outside and enjoy it while visiting. From world-class golf courses to secluded walking and horse trails, there are lots of ways to get moving. Many of these can be done individually or can involve the entire family.

For those interested in **saltwater** and **freshwater** fishing, keep in mind that anyone 16 and older must have the appropriate fishing license. There are several options to pick from. A saltwater license runs $12.50, or buy a temporary saltwater license good for 10 days for only $5. For Virginia residents, a combined, temporary freshwater/saltwater license can be purchased for $16. It costs $21 for non-residents. This temporary license is only good for five days. Licenses are sold at most parks where fishing is offered, plus area sporting goods stores, and even some large retail outlets which sell fishing equipment.

CAPITAL BIKE TRAIL

(**virginiacapitaltrail.org**) Take a bike ride on this new pedestrian and bike trail. It starts on the Colonial Parkway in Williamsburg, extends to Jamestown, and will eventually stretch 50 miles to Richmond along Route 5 once it is completed, traversing Virginia's past and present capitals. It's being completed in phases and only eight miles were finished and open to bikers at the time this book was written. Cyclists can park to pick up the trail at **Powhatan Creek Park** or behind Jamestown High School *(3751 John Tyler Highway)* where they can take a spur to reach the main trail. This is a National Recreation Trail designated by the U.S. Department of Interior and it's also part of the Transamerica Bike Route and East Coast Greenways.

COLONIAL HERITAGE

(6500 Arthur Hills Dr. ☎ 757.645.2000

🖰 colonialheritageclub.com) This semi-private golf club features a 175-acre par-72 championship course open to the public. There's also a large driving range with grass tees, a large arched chipping green with two bunkers, and a putting green. Green fees range from $35-$60 depending on the day of week and season. Clubs can be rented for 18-hole play for around $40 per set. There's a golf shop and a restaurant on-site.

COLONIAL NATIONAL HISTORICAL PARK AND THE COLONIAL PARKWAY

(From I-64, take exit 242A at Jamestown and 242B at Yorktown and follow signs to the parkway ☎ 757.898.2410

🖰 nps.gov/colo) The Colonial National Historical Park stretches from Yorktown to Jamestown, connecting these two to Colonial Williamsburg via its 23-mile Colonial Parkway. The three together form America's Historic Triangle, one of the most history-rich areas in the country.

The parkway begins at the **Yorktown Battlefield Visitor Center** parking area, heading west along the York River to Williamsburg. The road then turns south and then west to follow the James River, ending at **Historic Jamestowne**.

The three areas of the park span the time from pre-colonization to the winning of the country's independence. Historic Jamestowne is the actual site of the first permanent English settlement. The Yorktown Battlefield is where the last major battle of the Revolutionary War took place. There are also some Civil War sites within the park, like the **Yorktown**

National Cemetery where many Union and Confederate soldiers are buried.

The parkway is within the Colonial National Historical Park and maintained by the National Park Service. It winds through scenic wooded areas and along the shores of the James and York rivers. Drivers through the parkway will cross many small bridges, and there are designated areas to pull over to view nature or read historical markers.

The parkway is a grooved road, divided into three lanes in most areas. There are no lines on the road, only grooves. There is one lane in each direction and the center lane is for passing but only in designated areas based on signage, so be careful. The road is off limits to commercial vehicles and the speed limit is 45 miles per hour in most areas.

The park is home to many wild animals including deer, raccoon, opossum, red tail fox, bald eagles, wild turkey, and about 200 total species of birds. There are also many species of trees and plants, including wildflowers which blossom in the spring.

The parkway is popular with bikers and runners, especially the more secluded battlefield tour roads. Bicyclists are allowed on all paved roadways within the park except for the tunnel under Colonial Williamsburg. There is an alternate route here for both cyclists and pedestrians, who are also not allowed in the tunnel for safety reasons.

There are two tour roads in Yorktown, the seven-mile Battlefield Tour Road, marked by red arrows, and the nine-mile Encampment Tour Road, marked by yellow arrows.

The Battlefield Tour Road begins at the Yorktown Battlefield Visitor Center's parking lot. The Encampment Tour Road is nine miles long. It begins at Surrender Field. Both routes utilize other park roads and heavily traveled state highways, but the Encampment Tour road has less motor traffic.

Jamestown has three- and five-mile one-way scenic loops of the Island. These loops are open to pedestrians, cyclists, and motor vehicles. Buses, motor homes, or vehicles over five tons are prohibited on these small roads for safety reasons. To get to the loop drives, follow signs from the Historic Jamestowne parking lot. The speed limit on these roads is 15 miles per hour.

Be careful when driving along the parkway after dark, as there are many deer here that sometimes dart across the road. As far as possible, avoid stopping along the parkway at night. Locals themselves are wary of stopping on parkway lookouts after dark, because of a spate of unsolved murders that occurred here in the 1980s.

There is no charge to enter the parkway. There are charges to explore the Historic Jamestowne and the Yorktown Battlefield visitor's centers, however. Tourists can get into both sites for $10 total, with children under 16 admitted free of charge. Tickets are good for seven consecutive days from purchase to allow time to visit both sites. Both are open daily 9:00 a.m. to 5:00 p.m. except on Thanksgiving, Christmas, and New Year's days.

JAMES CITY COUNTY SKATE PARK
(5301 Longhill Rd.

 jccegov.com/recreation/parks/skate-park.html) This free skate park has 10,000 square feet of concrete jumps and ramps for skateboarders, in-line skaters, and scooters. The park features ramps, a hand rail, edges for grinding, and more. Children under 12 must be accompanied by an adult or an older teen. The park is run by James City County Parks and Recreation. Protective gear is highly recommended and use of the park is at your own risk. Open daily from 9:00 a.m. until dark year-round, weather permitting.

PLANT TOUR OF WOODY SPECIES AT THE COLLEGE OF WILLIAM AND MARY

(111 Jamestown Rd. 🖱 wm.edu/as/biology/planttour/index.php) This self-guided tour, which begins at the Sir Christopher Wren Building, winds through various locations on campus, where approximately 325 species and varieties of woody plants are located. Known as "The Baldwin Memorial Collection of Woody Species," the group is named after a longtime biology professor at the college, John T. Baldwin Jr. During his tenure from 1946 to 1974, Baldwin visited four continents. He would return to the campus with exotic species which were added to the college's landscape. The tour which showcases some of the collection begins and ends at the campus' Sir Christopher Wren Building. This is the oldest college building in the United States. A map outlining the tour can be downloaded from the Web site. A parking pass is essential in order to be able to park on the college campus without being ticketed. One can be obtained free of charge from the Information Center inside the Wren building.

REDOUBT PARK

(202 Quarterpath Rd. 🕿 757.259.3760) The park is just beyond the recreation center at Quarterpath Road. Opened in 2007, this small 22-acre city park includes two redoubts from a famous Civil War battle. It would appeal to history buffs or anyone who just wants a wide open space to explore. The park interprets and preserves the two redoubts, or earthwork forts, which were part of the Williamsburg Line. This line was a defensive fall-back line built to protect Richmond from the Union army, and the scene of a major battle in May of 1862. The park includes historical signs, walkways, and fencing highlighting the historic areas. Open daily dawn until dusk.

STONEHOUSE STABLES/LAKEWOOD TRAILS
(2116-A Forge Rd., Toano ☎ 757.566.9633

☝ **stonehousestables.com)** Explore wooded trails in the area by horseback. Guided tours range from one to three hours. Costs range from $65 to $275. They also offer themed rides for special occasions. Take a couples-only ride that winds up with a romantic picnic meal, or a birthday ride that ends with the presentation of a cake. Reservations are required. The trails are open daily except major holidays.

WALLER MILL PARK
(Rt. 645, Airport Rd. ☎ 757.259.3778 ☝ williamsburgva.gov)
Follow signs from Richmond Road to reach this 2,705-acre park, which was built around the city's reservoir in the early 1970s. It has a 286-acre lake stocked with striped and largemouth bass, crappie, blue gill, perch, catfish, and red-eared bream. Visitors can rent boats for fishing, canoeing, and kayaking for under $10, but electric motors and batteries cost extra. Fishing is also allowed from the park's pier at no charge. Anyone fishing must have a Virginia freshwater license. Pedal boats are another fun option for those who want to explore the lake.

There are various trails for ground exploration, including a two-mile asphalt biking and walking trail. There's a playground for children, and a **Lookout Tower** where visitors can get a different perspective of the area. Leave your bread crumbs at home because feeding the wildlife is prohibited here. Waller Mill includes a fenced dog park for those bringing their four-legged friends on vacation. The dog park has two separate areas for large and small canines.

Open daily except for Thanksgiving, Christmas Eve and Day, and New Year's Day.

WILLIAMSBURG NATIONAL GOLF CLUB

(3700 Centerville Rd. ☎ 800.826.5732 🖱 WNGC.com) This club now has two 18-hole courses, the Jamestown Course designed by Jack Nicklaus, and the newly opened Yorktown Course by Tom Clark. The Jamestown is a par-72 course rated four stars by *Golf Digest*. The Yorktown is a 7,000-yard championship course. Green fees range from $50 to $79. There is a pro instructor on-site. They have a nice all-natural driving range. There's also a golf shop and restaurant located here.

YORK RIVER STATE PARK

(5526 Riverview Rd. ☎ 757.566.3036 🖱 dcr.virginia.gov/state_parks/yor.shtml#location) Take exit 231B from I-64 to reach this 2,250-acre state park, located about 11 miles west of Williamsburg on the York River. It provides visitors with an up-close view of a coastal estuary, and has both freshwater and saltwater environments for nature watchers and fishermen, as well as more than 25 miles of hiking, biking, and equestrian trails. There are six trails, with two exclusively for mountain bikes (a six-mile for advanced riders and a two-mile for beginner/intermediate riders connected by a short half-mile trail.)

Park at the Croaker Landing entrance to fish in the York River. There is a $6 parking fee per car, but this is a good deal because it allows everyone in the car to fish from the 360-foot pier here without a saltwater fishing license (these cost $12.50 each). Young and old can cast their lines for croaker, spot, trout, and stripers. Those who are 16 and older and are fishing from the shore, a boat, or in the Taskinas Creek must have a saltwater license. The creek is home to many birds and other wildlife, and is part of the Chesapeake Bay National Estuarine Research Reserve. Largemouth bass and blue gill can be caught in the Woodstock Pond, but a Virginia freshwater fishing license is required to fish here.

The park includes a gift shop and a visitor's center where people can learn about the history and preservation of the York River and its wetlands areas. Paddleboats, canoes, jonboats, and kayaks can be rented for use on the creek and pond from April through October. Guided canoe and kayak trips are also offered Saturday and Sunday afternoons during the warmer months for around $10 per person or around $6 per person for a family of four or more. There is a $2 parking fee per vehicle on weekdays and $3 on weekends, at the main park entrance where the visitor's center is located, but you don't have to pay this fee if you've already paid at Croaker Landing.

Jamestown

Jamestown occupies a unique place of significance in U.S. history. It was the site of the first permanent English settlement in the United States, settled by Englishmen who arrived on ships way back in the early 17th century. They initially faced many hardships on this foreign soil due to their lack of skills, proper supplies, food and water. They also weren't familiar with the environment, not to mention the well-established Native Americans who'd inhabited the land for thousands of years. Many of the first settlers died and Jamestown was nearly abandoned several times, despite the arrival of more people, including women, and supplies from England. It was a long struggle, but eventually the settlers adapted to the surroundings and found ways to make a living off the land, primarily by raising tobacco. Soon afterward, the settlement began to expand into other parts of what is now Virginia.

HISTORICAL SIGNIFICANCE

Jamestown is the site of the first permanent English settlement in the United States. The settlers first arrived at this site on May 13, 1607 on three ships — the *Susan Constant, Discovery,* and *Godspeed.* A total of 105 men had left England, and 104 men arrived safely on the first voyage, with one man dying on the trip. They were led by Captain Christopher Newport. They arrived at Jamestown 13 years before the Pilgrims landed at Plymouth Rock in Massachusetts.

The voyage was sponsored by the Virginia Company of London, a group of investors interested in turning a profit. The company was chartered by King James I, in part to promote expansion of England abroad to compete with other European nations. He also wanted to find a northwest passage to the Orient.

The voyagers had spent close to five months at sea, including two weeks exploring inland waterways before landing at the site now called **Historic Jamestowne**. They chose the area for its deep water and because it seemed to offer a good defensive position. They came ashore one day after landing to begin the settlement, which they named after their king.

Problems began almost immediately, partially because most of the settlers were upper-class men rather than laborers and farmers. They did not have the skills and practical know-how to do much of what needed to be done. They also were unfamiliar with the environment and climate. It wasn't long before they ran short of both water and food, and many got sick or died.

They also began to have problems with the native people, as they had settled right in the midst of an area where more than 10,000 Powhatan Indians lived. Even though some trading took place between the native people who spoke Algonquin and the settlers, the relationship was strained.

In 1608, Captain Newport sailed back to England, returning to the settlement with more supplies and people, the first of a number of arrivals to replenish Jamestown. The first two women also arrived in the settlement that year, but men outnumbered women throughout the century.

In that same year, Captain John Smith was elected president of the governing council. He had played a key role in developing trade relations with the Indians. But when he returned to England because of an injury in 1609 never to return to Jamestown, warfare broke out between the natives and settlers. And once again, many settlers died of starvation and disease.

The settlers were close to abandoning Jamestown to sail back to England, when in 1610, a new batch of supplies and people arrived. They came under a second charter by the king calling for a governor to lead Virginia.

Early industries began in the settlement – glassmaking, wood production, and the manufacturing of pitch and tar and potash. None were very profitable until John Rolfe, who later married the legendary Pocahontas, introduced tobacco as a cash crop. Since tobacco farming required large plots of land and labor, the industry helped the colony to grow. By 1611, other settlements like Elizabeth City and Henrico were established. With expansion, the settlers continued to take more land from the Powhatan Indians and they also began to use indentured servants for labor.

By 1619, the first Africans were serving in the colony as indentured servants. They were brought from Ndongo in Angola where they had been captured by the Portuguese. By mid-century, colonists had begun the practice of owning African slaves for life, with slaves soon replacing indentured servants as the primary laborers.

The first representative government in British America was established at Jamestown in 1619 when a general assembly met.

A war with the Powhatan Indians followed in 1622 and two years later, the king dissolved the Virginia Company and established Virginia as a royal colony. Jamestown remained at the center of life in Virginia both politically and socially until 1699, when the capital of Virginia was moved to Williamsburg.

OVERVIEW AND RECOMMENDATIONS

There are two main routes to Jamestown from Williamsburg. Jamestown is located in James City County about six miles northwest of Colonial Williamsburg's Historic Area. Taking Jamestown Road off Route 199 is the fastest and most direct way to get there. The Colonial Parkway route is the most scenic and enjoyable though. The ten miles of parkway from Colonial Williamsburg to Jamestown make for a relaxing ride with fantastic views of the James River. There are many scenic lookout areas for pulling the car over. These are great spots for taking photos or watching for birds like bald eagles, osprey, and Great Blue Heron.

Jamestown Settlement is a living history museum recreated to show how the settlers traveled here from England and how they survived after landing. It also depicts how the area's Native American inhabitants lived. This is fun for adults and children alike, as there are hands-on activities. Guests can actually touch and feel things they see in the Powhatan Indian village, **James Fort** and on the three replica ships, which are open to climb aboard and explore. Keep in mind that Jamestown Settlement is entirely recreated, and not the site where the English settlers first lived. Besides the outdoor living history displays, there is a very large indoor gallery with hundreds of artifacts, several theaters showing educational films, gift shops, and a café serving a nice selection of lunch fare at reasonable prices.

To stand on the actual ground where the first settlers landed, the place to visit is **Historic Jamestowne**. Located just a few miles from Jamestown Settlement, this historic area consists of a visitor's center, the Archaearium museum with interactive exhibits, the actual archaeological excavation site of the original James Fort, and the **Glasshouse** with a live glassblowing exhibition. This is near the remains of the original settlement's glassmaking kiln and furnaces. The historic area is set in a beautiful location right on the river. It's a large wide-open space fun to explore.

Both Jamestown Settlement and Historic Jamestowne are suitable and recommended for all ages. Because of its many hands-on activities though, the Jamestown Settlement might be more popular with smaller children. On the other hand, adults and older children might prefer Historic Jamestowne because of its authenticity and the mysteries being unlocked there by archaeologists.

It's important to note here that unless you've purchased the America's Historic Triangle vacation package, there is separate admission for the Jamestown Settlement, which is run by the Jamestown-Yorktown Foundation, and for Historic Jamestowne, administered by the National Park Service and the APVA.

A fun and free activity at Jamestown is to take a ferry ride across the river to Surry County. It's a beautiful ride that couples, entire families, especially those with children, will most likely enjoy. Just remember that once you ride over, you have to also take the ferry to get back, and though it's a great experience, it is probably not for those who are in a hurry to get to the next destination.

THINGS TO DO AND SEE

Jamestown can be explored in a full day, but it's possible to stretch the visit to two days. This is especially true for those interested in exploring the many artifacts on display in greater depth, or those needing or preferring to move at a slower, more relaxed pace.

HISTORIC JAMESTOWNE

Historic Jamestowne includes the **Visitor's Center, Tercentenary Monument, Archaearium, Dale House Café, Glasshouse**, and original glasshouse ruins, island trail driving tour and most importantly, the original site of America's first permanent English settlement.

The first thing you will see as you head to the center is the Glasshouse and ruins parking area so stop here while entering or exiting. You do not pay park fees until entering the Visitor's Center. In this area, watch a costumed glassblower fire and shape vases and other objects from molten glass, which is heated in a large kiln.

The glasshouse includes a small attached outdoor gift shop where you can purchase beautiful glass vials, mugs, pitchers, and lamps. All the green glass objects sold here are made on-site. Glass is naturally green and that's the color of the glass made by the settlers. The colored glass sold here is blown in a Williamsburg studio using 17th-century tools and methods. Right down the hill from the glasshouse exhibition on the banks of the James, you can view the remnants of the original kiln and furnaces from 1608. Here German artisans first produced green glass. Markers at the site explain that glass-making was "America's First Industry."

Continuing on to the Historic Jamestowne **Visitor's Center**, which has a large free parking area and restroom facilities, visitors pay entrance fees covering all areas of Historic Jamestowne. This is the place to get free maps of the site and ask park rangers questions. After paying, you get a sticker allowing you to enter the historic settlement site and also the center's gallery and theater. The small gallery displays some original items found at the site and in the area, as well as recreated and replica items like the small wooden models of the ships that brought the first settlers to the area. The theater shows a 15-minute film telling the story of the settlement.

Exiting the rear entrance to the center, there is a walkway leading to a long footbridge. The bridge crosses a typical Virginia wetlands area and leads to the grounds of Historic Jamestowne. The first thing you'll see is the tall **Tercentenary Monument**. This monument was erected to commemorate the 300th anniversary of the settlement at Jamestown, and it stands more than 100 feet tall.

Moving through the walking tour to the fort area, the scenery itself is breathtaking, and there is an expansive view of the James River from this vantage point onward in the settlement area. It's easy to understand why the English picked this spot to make their home four centuries ago.

A statue of Pocahontas greets visitors outside the James Fort site. Inside the site you can go inside the **Jamestown Memorial Church**, which was also built for the 1907 anniversary, but erected around the original 1640s church tower. The tower is the only surviving structure from 17th-century Jamestown. Near the church is an active dig site where archaeologists continue to unearth foundations of original buildings and make new discoveries. There are also grave markers and other structures. A statue of Captain John Smith overlooks the river, and a model replica shows placement of buildings at the original settlement.

On the way to the Archaearium, visitors pass the **Dale House Café**. It has a large outdoor patio at the river's edge and a small inside dining area. It offers light lunch fare, drinks, and snacks.

The **Voorhees Archaearium Museum** is a gallery displaying a wide array of items found through the ongoing archaeological work in the original settlement area. The archaearium, the term for a building which displays an archaeological site while preserving it, opened in 2006. It was built on the ruins of the last Jamestown Statehouse, and there are several areas throughout the building where you can look through glass windows in the floor and see excavated foundations. In fact, an outline of the Statehouse is depicted throughout the museum in the carpeting.

Visitors here can learn about who the settlers were as human beings, including their life expectancy and how they survived. The museum also tells the story of how the settlement site was found by archaeologists, their discoveries since that time, and what they've learned about the original settlers and how they lived. Human skeletal remains exhumed from graves in the area are on display, as are items ranging from daggers and a full suit of armor to wine bottles and kitchen utensils.

There is a small gift shop area with souvenirs, books, and other collectibles at the exit to the building.

The tour continues on past the monument in the opposite direction of James Fort to **New Towne**. In this area, visitors can view the foundations of buildings constructed beyond the fort as the settlement expanded, and the ruins of an 18th-century mansion.

The tour winds up at the Visitor Center, where you can peruse the gift shop before exiting. Here you can buy books, replica items, toys, and other souvenirs.

Once back in the car, drive just past the parking area to enter the **Historic Jamestowne Island Trail**, which is also the western end of the Colonial Parkway. At the trail, the two-way parkway splits and makes a one-way loop around the island. There are actually two loops which run together so it's possible to do one or both. Driving the first loop only is a three-mile tour and both are five. Take your time as the speed limit is only 15 miles per hour.

Historic Jamestowne is administered jointly by the National Park Service and the Association for the Preservation of Virginia Antiquities. Special living history programs are presented on scheduled days, and short ranger-guided tours are available here some days based on staffing. Historic Jamestowne stays open daily 9:00 a.m. to 5:00 p.m. except Christmas and New Year's days. Admission is $10 and also covers admission to the **Yorktown Battlefield Visitor Center** for seven days from date of purchase.

JAMESTOWN SETTLEMENT
(Intersection of State Rt. 31 & Colonial Parkway
☎ **888.593.4682/757.253.4838 ☷ historyisfun.org)** Jamestown Settlement opened in 1957 to celebrate the 350th anniversary of the first permanent English settlement in America. New facilities, exhibits, and programs were recently added,

improving and expanding the museum in time for the 400th anniversary in 2007. The museum includes both indoor and outdoor exhibits, which take about three hours to explore. Outdoors, there is a large living history area, and inside, there are theaters, a gallery with 500-plus exhibits, and a good-sized café. You can begin your tour of the museum either indoors or outdoors, depending on the weather, time of day, or personal preference, but it really doesn't matter. In the summer, viewing the outdoor areas first is a good choice, so that by the time it becomes hotter, you can go inside to cool off and view the gallery's exhibits.

There are four main living history areas outside with costumed interpreters giving demonstrations and answering questions. These are James Fort, the Powhatan Indian village, the pier with three replica ships, and a seasonal riverfront discovery area. By exploring these exhibits, visitors get a close-up view of what conditions were like at Jamestown for the settlers, as well as the Powhatan Indians native to the area. All the buildings, furnishings, tools, and even the interpreters' costumes were recreated to be accurate based on historical accounts and knowledge.

Most people begin their outdoor tour at the Powhatan Indian village, but you can begin there or at James Fort. In the village see a ceremonial circle, a crop field, and the round houses made of saplings and reed mats. The village represents the way the Paspahegh Indians, the Powhatan group closest to Jamestown, once lived. Step inside the houses to see what they're like and touch the animal hides and furnishings. Depending on what's going on at any given time, there might even be interpreters giving demonstrations such as processing hides or preparing food. Participate in corn grinding and weaving natural fibers into cord if you feel adventurous. Children especially enjoy these hands-on opportunities, which can be educational and fun at the same time.

From the village, a walkway leads to James Fort and the pier. At the pier, replicas of the three original ships which the first settlers sailed on from England are on display: the *Susan Constant, Discovery, and Godspeed*. Climb aboard to explore the ships, which have interpreters to answer questions. Visitors can only explore below deck on the *Susan Constant*, the largest ship. She carried more than 50 passengers from England, and it's amazing to look around and imagine how they must have spent their four-and-a-half month journey to America. Going below deck and seeing the cramped quarters and the small size of the beds in nooks and on the floor is an eye-opening experience. See and touch canons, rope, pots, cooking utensils, even games that would have been played aboard the original ships. All the museum's areas are handicapped accessible except for the replica ships, although some handicapped persons not wheelchair-bound might be able to go on board. Everyone should keep in mind that there are narrow ramps leading from the pier up to each ship, but once up the ramps, there are steps down to the decks. To get below deck on the *Susan Constant*, the steps are steep going up and down so watch your step and small children closely.

Back up the hill to the right, visitors can stop by the seasonal riverfront discovery area, where there is a boat building exhibit. In warmer months, an interpreter will demonstrate how dugout canoes were made from logs. Try scraping out a canoe with an oyster shell.

At nearby James Fort, see how the early settlers lived. The fort includes rustic wattle-and-daub buildings including an Anglican church, storehouse, homes, and others. You can explore all the buildings inside and out, take a seat in the church or try on armor. Depending on what's going on at the time of your visit, you might see a musket firing demonstration, a blacksmith repairing metal objects, or an interpreter making wood products using 17th-century tools.

The indoor exhibits are divided into three areas. The first explores the state of the three cultures which converge on Jamestown prior to the 17th century. These include the Powhatan Indian culture, the Angolan villages from where the first African-Americans were taken, and the colonizing Europeans.

Exhibits in the second part of the gallery look at the relationship between the Powhatan Indians and the settlers, as well as how the African culture was affected by the slave trade. The third section examines the development and expansion of Jamestown politically, socially, and economically.

If at some point, you want to give your feet a rest, you can view the movie, *1607: A Nation Takes Root* in the museum's Robins Theater, or grab a quick snack or lunch in the café.

The cafeteria-style café serves a decent selection of sandwiches, soups and Brunswick stew, salads, and pizza. An adult can easily eat here for under $10, and there are also children's items.

The gift shop, located indoors on the main floor, sells books, prints, reproductions of some of the museum's artifacts, toys, games, jewelry, and other souvenirs.

The settlement is open daily except for Christmas and New Year's. Admission is $14 for adults, $6.50 for ages 6-12. Combination tickets for Jamestown Settlement and the **Yorktown Victory Center** are $19.25 for adults, $9.25 for children between 6 and 12 years of age. It is not necessary to visit both locations in the same day or even week.

JAMESTOWN-SCOTLAND FERRY
(Located at the end of Rt. 31,
⚓ virginiadot.org/travel/ferry-jamestown.asp) Close to one million vehicles are transported across the James River via the Jamestown-Scotland Ferry fleet annually, according to the Virginia Department of Transportation. It is a fun and free activity for the whole family to enjoy if the weather is nice, especially if there are small children along and there's no hurry to get anywhere.

Just remember that once at Surry County, you are going to have to take another ferry to get back. Once there though, **Chippokes Plantation State Park** *(695 Chippokes Park Rd.)* is a fun place to spend a few hours or the day. It features a living history exhibit of rural agriculture and is the site of one of the oldest working farms in the country. The park also has a visitor center, swimming complex, and trails for hiking or biking.

You can catch the ferry right up the road from the **Jamestown Settlement** at the end of Jamestown Rd. (Rt. 31). There are actually four ferry boats aptly named *Pocahontas, Surry, Williamsburg* and *Virginia*. The ride across the river to Surry County takes about 30 minutes, and once the ride is underway, passengers are allowed to get out of their cars and walk around unless the weather is really bad. Bring along some bread and let the kids throw it to the seagulls, or buy seed from machines onboard. You might also get lucky and see an American Bald Eagle as the James River is one of their major nesting areas east of the Mississippi. An estimated 500 adult and juvenile bald eagles visit the **James River National Wildlife Refuge** each year, according to the U.S. Fish and Wildlife Service.

Depending on exactly when you arrive at the ferry pier, expect anywhere from a 15-30 minute wait for the ferry, and it also takes some time to get all the cars properly parked on the boat. Also, keep in mind that some area residents use the ferry for their daily commute so traffic is heavier and waits are longer during peak traffic hours between 6:00–8:00 a.m. and 4:00–6:00 p.m. on weekdays. Due to heightened security measures, passengers may now be required to open their trunks or enclosed containers for screening. For posted ferry arrival times, which vary at different times of the year, or for vehicle size restrictions, visit the Web site above.

PLACES TO DINE AND SHOP ON THE WAY THERE

Besides the café at **Jamestown Settlement**, there aren't technically any restaurants in Jamestown because Jamestown isn't really a town anymore. There are two restaurants on Jamestown Road very close to Jamestown, though they are actually in Williamsburg. Also listed below is a nearby Christmas shop, very close to Jamestown attractions.

The scale for the dinner entrées is as follows: under $10 = ($), $10-$20 = ($$), and above $20 = ($$$).

CARROT TREE KITCHENS

(1782 Jamestown Rd. ☎ 757.229.0957 🖰 carrottreekitchens.com)
Opened in the mid 1990s in an old motel campground building
right off Jamestown Road, this quaint café isn't fancy from
the outside, but the food served is nothing short of superb.
The owners, who also run **Carrot Tree in the Cole Digges
House** at Yorktown, say the food is made from scratch daily.
There is a very fresh quality to everything from the Brunswick
stew to the crab cakes. The menu includes a variety of salads,
soups, sandwiches, and wraps, but definitely don't skip dessert.
All the baked goods are freshly made too. In fact, Debbi
Helsetch, who runs the Williamsburg restaurant while her
husband Glenn, manages the Yorktown location, opened this
first restaurant after running a commercial scratch bakery from
her garage for five years. Carrot cake, the first cake she ever
baked and sold, is one of the restaurant's most popular dessert
items. The key lime pie is also terrific. Both locations are
decorated with everything "carrot" from curtains, to wall hangings, figurines, and flags. The Williamsburg location is open
for lunch only, but the Yorktown restaurant also serves dinner
Thursday through Saturday, and has a high tea on Wednesdays
with guest speakers. There is limited seating for the tea so
reservations are recommended. Open daily except for major
holidays and the first week in January. *($)*

JAMESTOWN PIE COMPANY

(1804 Jamestown Rd. ☎ 757.229.7775 🖰 buyapie.com) This
pie shop is small and unassuming, and you'll pass it en route
to Jamestown if you go via Jamestown Road. It's basically a
takeout location, with only a couple tables outside near the
road for dining so it's better to pick up the food to take back

to the room. They offer a variety of nut pies like the Virginia Peanut Pie, fruit pies like Bumbleberry Peach, and Tart Red Cherry, depending on what's in season, and hot meat pot pies loaded with chicken, turkey or beef, mushrooms, and vegetables. The menu includes unusual varieties too, like the au gratin pot pie with shrimp, crab meat, scallops, and veggies. Typical takeout fare including pizza pies, salads, subs, and Stromboli is also available. This eatery also ships its nut pies and select fruit varieties for those who want more pie when they get back home. Open daily except major holidays. *($$)*

COOKE'S CHRISTMAS GIFTS & COLLECTIBLES

(1820 Jamestown Rd. ☎ 757.220.0099 🔲 cookesgardens.com) This local shop has been family owned and operated for more than 20 years. It's an interesting place to browse just to see the festive way it is decorated. There are large elves sitting on benches, Santas, and lots of Christmas trees loaded with ornaments. What sets this Christmas shop apart is its large selection of good quality artificial trees. They sell 50 styles in their own brand name, ranging from two- to 22-feet. They also ship all over the country. Besides trees and wreaths, the shop sells many quality collectibles like Steinbach nutcrackers, Annalee dolls, Mark Roberts Fairies and items by Christopher Radko, Kurt Adler, and Glitterazzi. There's a huge selection of ornaments, stockings, and other holiday decorations and supplies, plus year-round home décor items. This shop has some things not found at the other area Christmas shops. The shop is open daily.

Yorktown

Yorktown today, is an active community, as well as a quaint little tourist town of only 200 or so residents. It is part of the larger York County. Yorktown attracts about 500,000 visitors each year, many drawn by the historic attractions. Though modern in most respects, Yorktown has an important role in the history of the U.S.

HISTORICAL SIGNIFICANCE

In 1781, American troops led by General George Washington and French troops led by General Comte de Rochambeau trapped the British army led by General Lord Cornwallis at Yorktown. The American Revolution would end following this last significant battle of the war. Cornwallis and his troops formally surrendered to Washington's army on October 19, 1781. After the battle, many people in the colonies were still uncertain that their independence was real and minor skirmishes still occurred throughout the country between patriots and loyalists.

About 80 percent of the town of Yorktown was damaged during the siege, with many buildings destroyed. Prior to the war, it had been a prospering town of 250-300 buildings and 2,000 residents. Today it is an active community, as well as a quaint little tourist town of only 200 or so residents. It is part of the larger York County.

OVERVIEW AND RECOMMENDATIONS

Yorktown attracts about 500,000 visitors each year, many drawn by the historic attractions. Apart from the historical appeal, Yorktown is also a beach on the beautiful York River. Therefore during the warm months, there are lots of sunbathers and swimmers including both locals and tourists. The beach is fairly narrow though, so visitors shouldn't expect vast expanses of sand. There are also lots of boats moving along the water or docking at the piers here and people fishing as well. It's a great place to relax and people watch, get your feet wet, or just soak up the sun.

Riverwalk Landing is a fairly new area at the beach with shops and restaurants. It's a great place to stroll around, shop for a few hours, or to dine overlooking the river. There's a large two-tier parking deck at Riverwalk right off Water Street.

Parking is free. It is very convenient to park here as you can reach all the other Yorktown attractions from here via a free trolley which stops every 20 minutes or so. Just keep in mind that the lower deck has a three-hour parking limit. The **Watermen's Museum** celebrating the heritage of local watermen is also located along the shoreline.

The town is a fun place to explore on foot or by trolley, so don't limit your visit to the waterfront. Be sure to check out the **Victory Monument** up the hill from the river or to walk around the battlefield. It's a great place for a picnic or to fly a kite when it is windy.

Also don't miss the **Gallery at York Hall** and other great little shops on Main Street, as well as those scattered throughout the town. Or for a change of pace, explore some of the historic buildings.

The two main historical areas at Yorktown are the **Yorktown Victory Center** and the **Yorktown Battlefield**. Both sites have large free parking areas for those who prefer to drive their own cars. There are seven-mile and nine-mile self-guided driving tours at the battlefield to experience by car.

The battlefield is the actual site of the last major Revolutionary War battle, and where Lord Cornwallis surrendered to George Washington. The Victory Center is a museum about the American Revolution. It highlights the struggles of diverse, real people who lived during this tumultuous time. The center can easily be explored in two to three hours. The battlefield is more expansive. You could spend an hour or more just in the Visitor Center. Walking the sprawling battlefield grounds on your own can take much longer.

THINGS TO DO AND SEE

There is something for everyone in Yorktown. Explore the battlefield and other historic sites, soak up some sun on the beautiful stretch of beach, or explore the river by boat.

GRACE EPISCOPAL CHURCH
(111 Church St. ☎ 757.898.3261 ⛪ gracechurchyorktown.org)
This colonial church celebrated its 300th anniversary in 1997. It serves the York-Hampton Parish of the Episcopal Diocese of Southern Virginia. It survived two sieges during the Revolutionary War and a fire that destroyed much of the town in the early 1800s. The church's grounds are open to visitors. Tours of the building can also be requested by appointment. There are three Holy Eucharist services offered Sunday mornings and one on Wednesdays for anyone interested in attending a service. The church's parish house has a book and gift shop staffed by volunteers. It sells religious items, parish-related memorabilia, and seasonal gifts. Open Mondays through Saturdays from late morning to early afternoon.

HOT SPOT FISHING CHARTERS

(☎ 757.846.5546/757.867.8274

🖱 yorkcounty.gov/tourism/attractions.htm) Go fishing in the
bay or ocean with Captain Danny Forrest aboard the *Kate
Lynn Dawn*. Forrest is personable and his trips are child- and
family-friendly. He has a great deal of experience, having run
his charter business for 20 years. His boat can accommodate
up to six people. Costs range from $60 to $100 per person per
day depending on the type of fishing. The boat leaves out of a
dock in Poquoson in York County.

RIVERWALK LANDING

(Water St.) This fairly new development along the river
includes unique shops, several restaurants and places to grab an
ice cream or snack, two piers, and a performance area. There's
also a large two-tier parking deck right at Riverwalk Landing
off Water Street. Parking is free, although the lower deck has a
three-hour limit. Handicapped parking is available on the lower
level.

THE SCHOONER ALLIANCE

(Yorktown Sailing Charters, Riverwalk Landing ☎ 757.639.1233
🖱 schooneralliance.com) The *Alliance*, a 105-foot tall ship,
sails daily from a pier at **Riverwalk Landing** at Yorktown.
Onboard, you can get as involved as you'd like in deck activities. You can even help steer the ship, which sails mornings,
afternoons, and at sunset from May to November. The boat
stays on the York River and the sails last about two hours. A
trip costs around $30 for adults and $18 for children. Snacks
and beverages can be purchased onboard.

YORK COUNTY HISTORICAL MUSEUM AND THE MUSEUM ON MAIN

(301 Main St. and 408 Main St. ☎ 757.890.3508

📱 yorkcounty.gov/ychm) This free museum is staffed completely by volunteers so its hours and days of operation may vary. It displays relics from both the Revolutionary and Civil wars. It also has many other exhibits focusing on the history of the area, ranging from the days when Native Americans inhabited the land right up to the 20th century. The museum is located on the lower level of **York Hall**, but has also moved some of its exhibits to its easier-to-find Museum on Main. This location has special exhibits and houses special events. In general, the museum is open Tuesdays through Sundays until 3:30 p.m.

YORKTOWN TROLLEY

Ride this free trolley which operates in Historic Yorktown from 10:00 a.m. to 6:00 p.m. daily from mid-March to the beginning of November. The trolley stops in nine locations including **Riverwalk Landing**, the **Watermen's Museum,** the **Yorktown Victory Center, Yorktown Battlefield Visitor Center,** and the **Yorktown Victory Monument**. It takes the trolley about 20–25 minutes to complete its circuit.

YORKTOWN VICTORY MONUMENT

(📱 nps.gov/york/historyculture/vicmon.htm) This statue stands at the top of the hill overlooking the York River within the Colonial National Historical Park. It is adjacent to Comte de Grasse Street and there is a free parking area nearby. The inscriptions on the statue are interesting to read. Just five days after Cornwallis' surrender at Yorktown to the combined armies of France and America, the statue was commissioned by Congress to commemorate the victory as well as the

French-American alliance. The construction of the monument was not actually begun until 100 years later however, with its cornerstone laid for the Yorktown Centennial Celebration in 1881. It was completed in 1884, though the Liberty figure at the top of the statue was replaced after it was damaged by lightning in 1942. It had to be repaired again following another lightning strike in 1990.

WATERMEN'S MUSEUM

(309 Water St. ☎ 757.887.2641 ⬤ watermens.org) This small non-profit museum is located right along the waterfront in Yorktown. It pays homage to the men and women who, for many generations, have earned their livelihood from the natural resources like blue crabs, oysters, and clams, in the Chesapeake Bay and its tributaries. These commercial fishermen today are still called "watermen" in the area, though their numbers have drastically decreased along with the once abundant fish and shellfish. Through exhibits, photos, and displays the museum recognizes the watermen's contributions to the region, which date back to the American Revolution. Watermen were said to have helped the French fleet to corner British ships near the end of the war in 1781. Open daily except Mondays from May through Thanksgiving, and on weekends only the rest of the year. Admission is $4 for adults and $1 for students from kindergarten to the 12th grade.

YORKTOWN BATTLEFIELD AND VISITOR CENTER

(1000 Colonial Parkway ☎ 757.898.2410 ⬤ nps.gov/colo) There are lots of ways to explore the various elements of the Yorktown Battlefield which sits high on a hill overlooking the river. This national park site includes a Visitor Center with historical exhibits, the sprawling battlefield grounds, roads which wind through historical areas for the driving tour, and the **Victory Monument**. The **Nelson House** located a short distance away on Main Street, **Moore House**, and the **Yorktown National Cemetery** are also maintained by the National Park Service.

Visitors have a lot of freedom in exploring the battlefield grounds and can walk or drive various areas at their leisure, as well as take a self-guided town tour. The monument is adjacent to the battlefield on a state-maintained road, and both the monument and grounds can be explored without paying admission. An admission fee is not required until entering the Visitor Center, although it is very reasonable.

For those who desire a more structured tour, ranger-guided tours are given at intervals at the Visitor Center. These are all around 30 minutes long and include a Siege Line Tour, Town Tour, and Artillery Demonstrations (summer only). The center is a great place to begin your tour of the park. It features a large free parking area and restroom facilities, plus park rangers and guides there also provide information.

At the center, visitors can learn about the areas of the battlefield and their significance. A movie of about 15 minutes called the *Siege of Yorktown* gives an overview of the events of 1781. There are also historical exhibits showing artifacts from the battle. There are even tents used by George Washington's army.

The center has a nice gift shop to purchase reproduction items and other souvenirs. You can also buy audio tapes for the driving tours.

Tours of the Nelson and Moore houses are offered daily in the afternoons in the summer. Call to check hours and days of the tours during other times of the year. The Nelson House is the 18-century home of Thomas Nelson Jr., a signer of the Declaration of Independence and Yorktown's most fierce and beloved patriot. He commanded the Virginia Militia during the war. He also served as a member of the Continental Congress, the state legislature and was a governor of Virginia. He is buried at **Grace Episcopal Church** in Yorktown.

The home was used in the Civil War as a Confederate hospital, and remained in the Nelson family until the early 1900s. It is one of Virginia's finest examples of Georgian architecture. Today the home is still primarily original. It is decorated with reproduction furniture and accessories, as well as a few period pieces. Tours cover the first floor only.

The Moore House is where negotiations to end the war took place on October 17, 1781. It was restored by the National Park Service in the early 1930s and today is furnished with colonial décor. It is a stop on the scenic seven-mile driving tour which winds through quiet wooded areas along the siege lines and encampment areas of the last battle of the Revolution.

The site of Washington's headquarters, the **American Artillery Park**, a French cemetery **Surrender Field**, and the **Yorktown National Cemetery** are some of the other sites on the two driving tours. The national cemetery has over 2,000 graves of Civil War soldiers, primarily Union soldiers from an 1862 campaign.

The battlefield offers a Junior Ranger Program for children 12 years and under. Parents can purchase a booklet for their child in the gift shop that can be completed while the family explores the park. This is a good way for families to make their park visit more structured and a learning experience while also having fun. It takes about two hours to complete the booklet and children receive a certificate and a patch when they are finished.

Open daily 9:00 a.m. to 5:00 p.m. except on Christmas and New Year's. Admission is $5 for those 17 and older, and is good for seven consecutive days. Visitors may also purchase a Jamestown-Yorktown Passport for $10 which gets them into the Visitor Center at Yorktown as well as **Historic Jamestowne** for the same time period.

YORKTOWN VICTORY CENTER

(Route 1020 ☎ 757.253.4838 ⬇ historyisfun.org) You can easily walk around this center in an hour or two, even if you go to the theater. It is primarily a museum with many indoor exhibits, although there are two recreated outdoor areas. One area depicts a Continental Army encampment and the other, a 1780s farm showing post-war living conditions. All the buildings, furnishings, tools, and even the interpreters' costumes in these areas are made to be accurate based on historical accounts and knowledge.

The center's tour begins with a walkway with timeline markers describing the events that led up to the Revolutionary War. The walkway leads to and continues inside a large museum of indoor exhibits, which has several galleries with different exhibits. One has a replica of and examines the importance of the Declaration of Independence. Another explores the battleships sunk in the York River. A film titled *A Time of Revolution* is shown every 30 minutes in the gallery's Richard S. Reynolds Foundation Theater.

One of the most interesting areas of the museum is the Witnesses to Revolution Gallery. Here visitors listen to the accounts of real men and women from various backgrounds who lived at the time of the Revolution. Through life-sized sculptures of the persons, paintings, and oral recordings, visitors get to hear the accounts of people like Jehu Grant, a Rhode Island slave who ran away from his master to join the Continental Army in 1777; Jacob Ellegood, a Virginian who formed a regiment of 600 men loyal to England; and Little Abraham, a Mohawk chief who tried to keep his people out of the war.

After viewing the museum, proceed outdoors to the encampment to see several interpreters dressed as soldiers firing a canon and preparing meals. You can step inside replica tents, learn about medical practices used during the war, or try on a uniform. Depending on the time and day of your visit, you could have the chance to join an artillery crew or drill with wooden muskets.

Then walk over to the recreated colonial farm where you can see gardens with tobacco, flax, cotton, corn, and other vegetables and herbs grown on Virginia farms following the Revolution. You can see turkeys in the farm area and peek inside a kitchen where stews and pies may be cooking. There are sometimes opportunities to help water the garden with a hollowed gourd, grind spices, or break "flax."

The gift shop sells lots of souvenirs like tee-shirts, jewelry, home décor, pottery, and glass pieces. There are also replica items including wooden toys, coins, and Revolutionary War paper money. There is a great selection of books on George Washington and other significant figures of the Revolution.

Open daily except for Christmas and New Year's. Admission is $14 for adults, $6.50 for children between the ages 6–12. Combination tickets for the **Yorktown Victory Center** and **Jamestown Settlement** are $19.25 for adults and $9.25 for 6–12 year olds. Ticket holders do not have to visit both locations in the same day or week.

RESTAURANTS

There are a number of dining options in Yorktown whether you want pizza and fries or an exquisite gourmet meal. Many of the restaurants offer views of the river. Others offer unique experiences. At **Carrot Tree**, for example, guests can dine in Yorktown's oldest home. Besides the restaurants listed here, keep in mind that the **Duke of York Hotel** on the beach also offers breakfast, lunch, and dinner.

The scale for the dinner entrées is as follows: under $10 = ($), $10-$20 = ($$), and above $20 = ($$$).

THE BEACH DELLY

(524 Water St. ☎ 757.886.5890) This small diner is located on Water Street past **Riverwalk Landing** and has a good beach view. It serves homemade pizza, deli sandwiches, subs, hand-cut fries, and homemade desserts. Open daily for lunch and dinner. Drinks served here include beer and wine. *($)*

CARROT TREE IN THE COLE DIGGES HOUSE

(411 Main St. ☎ 757.988.1999 🖋 carrottreekitchens.com) Guests here will dine in Yorktown's oldest home, set in the historic **Cole Digges House** built around 1720. The restaurant, which has another location in Williamsburg near Jamestown, serves freshly prepared delicious food. Open for lunch daily and for dinner Thursdays through Saturdays. *($$)*

NICKS RIVERWALK RESTAURANT
(323 Water St., Suite A-1 ☎ 757.875.1522

🖱 **riverwalkrestaurant.net)** This waterfront establishment overlooking the river includes two areas, the more casual **Rivah Café** *($$)* and the formal **Riverwalk Dining Room** *($$$)*. Dine outside on the patio if the weather is nice, or indoors by a window overlooking the York River, in either the café or dining room. They both serve lunch and dinner and each have their own menus. Some dishes are available for lunch and dinner like the café's Triple Crab, a crabcake topped with crab salad served with a mug of she crab soup. A decent-sized wrap-around bar sells daiquiris, bellinis, margaritas, draft beers, lagers, ales, and over a dozen wines by the glass or bottle.

YORKTOWN PUB
(540 Water St. ☎ 757.886.9964) Enjoy a magnificent view of the York River while dining at this gathering spot, a favorite with the locals. The menu features homemade soups, sandwiches, local seafood selections, burgers, nachos, and salads. There's a full bar and the pub is open late until 2.00 a.m. on Fridays and Saturdays. Open daily for lunch and dinner. *($)*

SHOPPING

Definitely browse the shops at **Riverwalk Landing**, but don't forget to venture beyond the beach area to explore the shops dispersed elsewhere in the historic village. You'll find unique art, antiques, colonial treasures, and a whole lot more.

PERIOD DESIGNS

(401 Main St. ☎ 757.886.9482 ✆ perioddesigns.com) This shop features English Delft, slipware, and contemporary pieces by ceramic artist Michelle Erickson. She specializes in 17th- and 18th-century English ceramic techniques. Her works for sale include decorative plates, bowls, vases, figurines, and other unique intricately finished ceramic objects. The shop also sells European and American antiques from the collection of Robert Hunter, whose specialty is English ceramics.

STARS & STRIPES FOREVER

(Riverwalk Landing ☎ 757.898.0288) See lots of red, white, and blue, plus stars and stripes in this patriotic store adjoining **Nicks Riverwalk Restaurant**. Besides typical souvenirs, shoppers will find political memorabilia, Democrat and Republican items, campaign pins, tee-shirts, hats, flags, bumper stickers, books, children's items, jewelry, and more.

THE GALLERY AT YORK HALL

(301 Main St. ☎ 757.890.4490 ✆ yorktown.gov/cyc) Featuring the work of approximately 150 area artists, this shop has a large selection of original paintings and art. Many pieces focus on the area's natural treasures and history. Paintings found here feature shells, birds, boats, colonial scenes, and more. Shoppers will also find pottery and glass items, handmade jewelry, enameled dishes, textile pieces such as quilts, and wooden pieces like miniature birdhouse ornaments. Other items that can be bought include vases, linens, wall hangings, and other objects for decorating your home. The shop also sells many seasonal and holiday items. The gallery holds special exhibits and shows throughout the year, including a quilt exhibit in the spring and a pottery exhibit in the fall. While in the building, visitors may want to check out the **York County Historical Museum's** exhibit in the lower level if open. The gallery is open daily except Mondays.

NANCY THOMAS GALLERY

(145 Ballard St. ☎ 877.645.0601 🖱 nancythomas.com) Folk art fans will love this small shop featuring the work of nationally renowned artist Nancy Thomas. Items range from jewelry pieces to large wall hangings. There are pretty hooked rugs created by Thomas designed in collaboration with artist Claire Murray. Thomas promotes the works of other artists like Matt Sesow and Michael Banks in her gallery as well. Open houses and special events are planned throughout the year. There is also a small café where gourmet food is offered during special events by chef Teresa King of **Fit for a King** catering. Don't miss a chance to try her roasted sweet potato salad with bacon, pecans, and maple vinaigrette. The gallery is open daily; the café for special events only.

STUDIO FORAY

(323 Water St. Suite A4 ☎ 757.969.1094 🖱 studioforay.com) You'll find beads galore at this shop at **Riverwalk Landing**. It sells beads, natural stones, and Czech glass for jewelry making. They also sell handmade jewelry boards and finished jewelry pieces. Custom pieces can be ordered. Open daily with some reduced hours in winter.

SWAN TAVERN ANTIQUES

(300 Main St. ☎ 757.898.3033 🖱 antiquesatswantavern.com) This shop specializes in fine 18th-century and early 19th-century furniture and accessories. It offers grandfather clocks, mirrors, rugs, art, pottery, silver, china, and much more. The shops stays open daily.

VICCELLIO GOLDSMITH

(325 Water St. ☎ 757.890.2162 🖱 viccelliogoldsmith.com)
Located at **Riverwalk Landing**, this shop is run by J. Henry "Hank" Viccellio, a master goldsmith and precious metals' craftsman. Customers can choose from beautiful one-of-a-kind jewelry pieces in gold and silver, many featuring precious gems and stones. The shop also sells limited edition jewelry items like the Jamestown Locket, which is hand engraved in 18-karat gold in Birmingham, England. Open daily.

YORKTOWN SHOPPE LTD. ✪ Must See!

(402 Main St. ☎ 757.898.2984 🖱 yorktownshoppe.com) This shop makes you feel like you're stepping back in time, which might be because it's located in a building constructed in 1881. George Sage, one of the shop's owners, is friendly to talk to and it's clear he takes pride in the unique items found in his store. Most are made locally or in the country. Shoppers here can buy replicas of many of the colonial houses they see in Williamsburg and Yorktown. They are done in authentic colors and to scale, according to Sage. The shop also houses hand-made metal balance toys, although they are much more show pieces than toys for children, and come in various themes, from colonial to nautical. There are many other items as well, which are made from wood, leather, brass, tin, and pewter. Shoppers will find some apparel also, ranging from handcrafted aprons and tapestry vests to bonnets and tri-corner hats, plus clothing for dolls. The shop is open daily.

PLACES TO STAY

There are a very limited number of places to spend the night if you want to stay right in the historic Yorktown area on the river. Fortunately the available options do represent variety. They include a riverfront hotel where all rooms have views of the river, several bed and breakfasts, and even a quaint cottage perfect for a romantic getaway for two. For those wishing to stay outside of the village, also included is a nearby, easy-to-get-to motel. Standard room rate in peak season starts at under $100 = ($), $100-$200 = ($$), and above $200 = ($$$).

DUKE OF YORK HOTEL

(**508 Water St.** ☎ **757.898.3232** ⬤ **dukeofyorkmotel.com**) All the rooms in this older, family-run hotel feature waterfront views of the York River. Some have private patios and others open on to the grounds. The hotel's **Island Café** serves breakfast, lunch, and dinner and offers a river view as well. The hotel has a large pool. All rooms include cable television with HBO and hair dryers. There is also one room featuring a two-person Jacuzzi. The hotel has ample free parking and is on the free Yorktown Trolley's route. Both smoking and non-smoking rooms are available. *($)*

MARL INN B&B

(**220 Church St.** ☎ **757.898.3859** ⬤ **marlinnbandb.com**) This inn is located near all of Yorktown's points of interest and about two blocks from **Riverwalk Landing**. It is the private residence of an ancestor of Thomas Nelson Jr., a signer of the Declaration of Independence. Its accommodations, one room and three suites, all have private baths and private outdoor entrances. They also have televisions and VCRs, plus a movie library. Suites have a full kitchen and the room includes a partial kitchen with microwave, refrigerator, and dishes. A complimentary full breakfast is served in the dining area or on the patio. However, those on a budget can forgo the full breakfast and opt for the value package. With this package, the room or suite is stocked with milk, cereal, freshly baked bread, and other breakfast items for a substantial rate discount. Children are welcome and there are some limited accommodations for pets. No smoking is allowed. *($$)*

THE MOSS GUEST COTTAGE

(224 Nelson St. ☎ 757.715.2007 🖰 mossguestcottage.com) Guests can stay in the heart of the Yorktown village in this quaint one-bedroom guest cottage. The cottage has a small fully equipped kitchen, plus a combined living room and dining area and a small breakfast nook. The cottage is equipped with a washer and dryer, cable television, a DVD player and books, puzzles, and movies. It accommodates two adults and is ideal for couples who want to get away for a weekend or longer. Smoking is not allowed here. *($$)*

YORK RIVER INN B&B

(209 Ambler St. ☎ 757.887.8800/800.884.7003 🖰 yorkriverinn.com) This bed and breakfast sits high on a hill overlooking the York River on the opposite side of the bridge from **Riverwalk Landing**. It offers three guestrooms, each accommodating two adults, with private bathrooms. The Presidents' Room is decorated with artifacts from seven U.S. presidents and has a private deck overlooking the river. Amenities include Wi-Fi, cable television, VCRs, comfortable bathrobes and slippers, lighted make-up mirrors, hair dryers, and more. There is a common living room area with a sofa, chairs, and large selection of reading materials. There is also a shared deck with patio chairs. The refrigerator is fully stocked for guests and snacks are also set out on the dining table. A knowledgeable innkeeper can answer guests' questions and give them information about the area. He also prepares a full breakfast of items like spinach and artichoke pie, Southern cinnamon toast, poached pears and cranberries, and shrimp and scallop ceviche. Guest rooms are located on the second and third floors and are accessible only by stairs. Smoking is allowed on the decks but not indoors. No children or pets are allowed. *($$)*

YORKTOWN MOTOR LODGE
(8829 George Washington Memorial Hwy.
☎ **757.898.5451/800.950.4003** 🖰 **yorktownmotorlodge.com)**
This one-story motel is located outside of the Yorktown village and is not in the beach area; however, it has been newly remodeled and is a good option for guests who prefer not to be right in the tourist area. The motel is easy to get to as it is located right off Route 17, a ten-minute drive from the historic area and the beach. Rooms include phones, cable television, free high-speed Internet access, alarm clocks, coffee makers, hair dryers, microwaves, and refrigerators. Your stay includes a complimentary continental breakfast. There is a large outdoor pool. No pets are allowed at the lodge. *($)*

Day Trips and Excursions

Williamsburg is in close proximity to other interesting places. This section is designed to give guests spending several days or more in Williamsburg some additional travel ideas. Here two locations within a short drive of Williamsburg have been highlighted.

Included in the chapter are two wonderful museums in Newport News, less than 30 minutes away from Williamsburg, where visitors can easily spend a day. Then there are plenty of unique dining, shopping, and activities for a one- to two-day visit to historic Gloucester County, across the river from Yorktown.

SPENDING A DAY IN NEWPORT NEWS

Spend the morning visiting the museum of your choice, the **Mariner's Museum** or the **Virginia Living Museum**. They are only minutes apart so you might want to decide based on the weather. The Mariner's Museum is primarily indoors, while a good deal of the Virginia Living Museum is outdoors. Small children will probably prefer the latter because of all the animals.

Following the museum visit, have lunch at the nearby **Patrick Henry Mall. Red Robin** is a convenient place for families to eat. Or try **Bailey's** if you want to catch up on a sporting event or wind down with an alcoholic beverage.

Spend the afternoon visiting the other museums, or just browsing around the numerous shops at the mall. There's something for every member of the family, from a spa and salons to sporting goods to a toy store.

If you want to grab a quick dinner on the way back to Williamsburg, **Plaza Azteca** is near the mall. The service is quick and the Mexican-American food served here is both tasty and very reasonably priced. It's a good place for a family to dine without breaking the bank.

MARINER'S MUSEUM

(100 Museum Dr. ☎ 757.596.2222 🖰 mariner.org) This is one of the world's largest maritime museums celebrating the history of important waterways around the world, their people, boats, and in general all things nautical. Many of the museum's 35,000 exhibits focus on the unique history of the Chesapeake Bay region and its role in the Revolutionary and Civil wars. About two-thirds of the exhibits are 3-D objects like small boats and ship's models, and the other third are paintings. Besides its permanent collections, there are visiting exhibits which vary, as well as online exhibits to check out at any time. A huge new USS Monitor Center wing opened in 2007, featuring an interactive exhibit on the *Monitor* and the CSS *Virginia*. These two ironclad vessels battled in nearby Hampton Roads during the Civil War. It takes about two hours to walk through the museum. The **Compass Café** located here sells sandwiches, soups, and salads, and there is also a gift shop with many nautical items. If the weather is nice, the surrounding 550-acre park on Lake Maury is a great place for a stroll or an afternoon picnic. Open daily except Thanksgiving and Christmas days. Admission is around $15 for adults, with discounts offered for children between 6–12 years, seniors, military personnel, and students. Children 5 years and under get in free.

PLAZA AZTECA

(12755 Jefferson Ave. ☎ 757.833.0271 🖱 plazaazteca.com)
Diners can eat fairly inexpensively and quickly here. The food
is pretty good Americanized Mexican cuisine. Diners are
served tortilla chips and salsa to snack on while waiting. The
menu includes lots of quesadillas, burritos and fajitas, plus
salads, and vegetarian options. There is a children's menu. *($)*

PATRICK HENRY MALL

(12300 Jefferson Ave. ☎ 757.249.4305
🖱 shoppatrickhenrymall.com) This large indoor shopping mall
has lots of great places to shop. The larger stores include
Macy's, Dillard's, JC Penney, and a new Dick's Sporting Goods.
Shoppers will find trendy clothing shops like New York &
Company, Old Navy, PacSun, American Eagle Outfitters, Tillys,
and others. There's a Border's Book & Music store, a Radio
Shack, hair salons, and stores that sell jewelry, shoes, and toys.
There are also lots of places to eat like **Red Robin, Bailey's
Pub & Grille, Ruby Tuesday,** and **Chipotle Mexican Grille**.

VIRGINIA LIVING MUSEUM

(524 J. Clyde Morris Blvd. ☎ 757.595.1900 🖱 thevlm.org) This
is a great spot to take children because you can move through
it at your own pace or theirs. It is much like a zoo, but only
has animals native to Virginia and focuses on education. There
are more than 200 animals, from bobcats and raccoons, to the
canebrake rattlesnake and the moon jellyfish. All the plants
used in the exhibits and gardens are native to the state too.
Both the animals and plants represent various Virginia habitats,
from the mountains to the forests to the coast. You can view
animals like otters and wolves in natural exhibits as you wind

through outdoor trails and bridges. There are turtles and other fauna in a large pond and there is also a bird aviary. Animals like bats and other nocturnal creatures, reptiles, and fish are found indoors.

A planetarium with a 30-foot projection dome theater shows daily programs targeted to varying age groups. In the observatory, you can view the sky through telescopes and other instruments if the weather is good. Visitors concerned with the environment can learn to live, build and garden "green" in the new Living Green House and Conservation Garden. There are usually special summer exhibits to interest children and families, like the robotic dinosaur exhibit in 2010. Museum admission runs around $15 for adults with discounts for children 3-12. Entry is free for children 2 years and under.

EXPLORING GLOUCESTER – A UNIQUE PLACE

This rural county is directly across the York River from Yorktown. You will see it as you drive along the river on the Colonial Parkway. It's a great excursion for those who want to visit some place unique and off the beaten path. On the way there from York County, visitors cross the George P. Coleman Memorial Bridge, the world's largest double swing-span bridge. There's a $2 toll (less if you have an E-Z Pass) going toward Gloucester, but none traveling the other direction so you only pay one way.

The county was established in 1651 and has an interesting yet little-known history outside of the region. Its Gloucester Point area was the site of a small battle that followed the victory at Yorktown in 1781. Thomas Jefferson and George Washington both frequently visited the county, and Washington was said to have bet on horses which raced at Seawell's Tavern, a colonial tavern off Route 17. The county is also the birthplace of Walter Reed, and was once home to a large daffodil industry. The flowers were shipped by steam ships to major cities like Baltimore and New York. It is still home to a thriving daffodil business and an annual Daffodil Festival is held each spring.

Gloucester's Court House area is the best place to start your visit. You can park along Main Street *(Business Rt. 17)* or on several side streets at no charge, and browse through a number of quaint, local one-of-a-kind shops. Walk over to the **Colonial Court Green**, where the 18th-century Colonial Courthouse is still in use today. Four historic buildings, including a debtor's prison, are open to visitors. Stop at the Visitor Center for information and to gain access to the other buildings. Visitors can also pick up brochures on other places to visit in Gloucester. There is a tiny gift shop that sells books and souvenirs.

Some historical sites to explore in the county include two colonial churches, Abingdon Episcopal and Ware Episcopal churches, the ruins of **Rosewell**, a grand mansion frequented by Thomas Jefferson and Walter Reed's birthplace. Other interesting places to explore are described below in greater detail.

BRENT AND BECKY'S BULBS SHOPPE
(7900 Daffodil Lane ☎ 877.661.2852
🖱 brentandbeckysbulbs.com) Turn on Rt. 14 off Main Street, and in just a few miles, you'll see a sign for Brent and Becky's Bulbs Bulb Shoppe. This shop is a must-see for plant enthusiasts, especially in the spring, when you can see hundreds of varieties of daffodils in bloom. Owners Brent and Becky Heath are well known around the country as bulb experts

because of their popular bulb catalogues. They can help you pick the right bulbs for your home's climate or answer any questions you might have about gardening.

GLOUCESTER POINT BEACH PARK

(1255 Greate Rd., Gloucester Point ☎ 804.642.9474
☗ gloucester.va.info/pr/parks/gpb.htm) This beach is located right under the George P. Coleman Memorial Bridge across the river from Yorktown. It is usually not too crowded and it's pretty isolated from commercial establishments and traffic. There's a playground for small children, a picnic area, and a long pier for fishing or catching blue crab in the York River. During the busy beach months, refreshments are sold in the beach house, where restroom facilities and outdoor showers are provided. For safety's sake, visitors planning to swim should be sure to observe posted signs. Swimming is prohibited at certain spots of the beach.

INN AT WARNER HALL

(4750 Warner Hall Rd. ☎ 804.695.9565/800.331.2720
☗ warnerhall.com) Stay in this elegant country inn on the Severn River, built in 1642 by George Washington's great, great grandfather, Augustine Warner. Washington often visited here to see his grandparents. Warner's descendants also include Robert E. Lee, famous explorer Meriwether Lewis, and Queen Elizabeth II who visited the home in her first U.S. trip in 1957. Nathaniel Bacon also retreated to the home after burning Jamestown.

Guests here can stay in one of 11 charming rooms decorated tastefully with period antiques, yet equipped with all the modern amenities. Rooms have private baths, flat screen televisions, even hair dryers, plus guests are pampered with terry robes, down comforters, and luxurious bath products. Rooms include a full breakfast served on the glass-enclosed porch overlooking the river. Homemade snacks and beverages are also complimentary all day. The inn includes a number of common rooms open to guests including a library with one of the oldest fireplaces in Virginia and a drawing room.

There are gardens, pastures, stables, and a pier for guests to explore on the 38-acre estate. To just kick back and relax, there's a boathouse with a Jacuzzi. Dinner is a fine five-course meal prepared by Chef Eric Garcia. Butter braised lobster with lemon infused basmati rice and Bok Choy is just one of the entrée selections. Boxed lunches prepared by the chef can be purchased for about $10. Dinner, however, will cost about seven times that. Reservations are required for lodging and for dinner, which is available Fridays and Saturdays to guests and non-guests. Check the inn's web site for weekend getaway and other specials. *($$$)*

RIVER'S INN
(8109 Yacht Haven Rd., Gloucester Point ☎ 804.642.6161 ⬤ riversinnrestaurant.com) Dine on the casual crab deck where you can crack and eat steamed blue crabs by the bucket. Or for a fine dining experience, eat indoors in the restaurant. There are great views of the York River to be had from either place. *($$)*

VIRGINIA INSTITUTE OF MARINE SCIENCE (VIMS)
(The College of William and Mary, 1208 Greate Rd., Gloucester Point ☎ 804.684.7000 ⬤ vims.edu) This graduate school of the College of William and Mary is situated on the beach area of Gloucester Point across the York River from Yorktown. It

has a nice lobby and small aquarium area which is open to the public at no charge on weekdays. The aquarium showcases the saltwater fish, turtles, and other rich marine life of the river and bay. A touch tank allows visitors to explore shellfish, horseshoe and blue crabs, and fish like puffers and flounder up close. The institute also offers public tours of its research facilities and teaching marsh on Friday mornings during the summer at no charge. The one-and-a-half-hour tours are geared toward older children and adults, and reservations are required (☎ *804.684.7846).* VIMS attracts students and scientists from around the world, as it conducts extensive research in coastal ocean and estuarine science. Its research often affects public policies and regulations to ensure the protection of marine life.

WHITLEY'S PEANUT FACTORY

**(1977 George Washington Memorial Hwy. ☎ 804.642.1975
🖮 whitleyspeanut.com)** Anyone who loves peanuts should consider putting this shop on their itinerary. The shop is located a few from the bridge on the right off Route 17. The peanuts are hand cooked the old fashioned way at a local warehouse. These peanuts are crisp and fresh and come in flavors to suit just about every taste, whether it's spicy or sweet. Butter toffee and Classic Chesapeake with crab seasoning are just two of the choices. The shop also sells other gourmet nuts, nut candies, natural peanut butter, boiled and raw peanuts, Virginia hams, sweet potato biscuits with Virginia ham, and more. Shelled nuts can be purchased by the tin or case. Special gift packs and tins are offered for the holidays. Shipping service is offered as well. Whitley's also has a shop in Williamsburg *(1351 Richmond Rd.).*

THE WILD RABBIT CAFÉ

(6604 Main St., Gloucester ☎ 804.694.5100) This spacious local café in the village serves delicious panini, wraps, sandwiches, and homemade quiches. In the morning, you can try the breakfast casserole, a breakfast panini with eggs and bacon, or a freshly baked muffin, scone, or bagel. They serve salads and different soups each day. Soups and quiches are served with fresh-baked zucchini bread. A children's menu features items like macaroni and cheese, cheese pizza, peanut butter and jelly sandwiches, and cheese panini. The café is open daily. *($)*

Shops in Colonial Williamsburg are run by costumed interpreters who are usually very knowledgeable about the items they sell and colonial history in general.

Sample Itineraries

Whether you're looking for quality family time or planning a romantic getaway for two, here are some tailor-made itineraries designed by the author to help you optimize vacation time. Use as they are or customize to suit your own style.

A DAY OF HIS AND HER INDULGENCES IN WILLIAMSBURG

Morning — Enjoy your complimentary breakfast at the **Fife and Drum Inn**, then together explore the **Abby Aldrich Rockefeller Folk Art Museum** at Colonial Williamsburg. Lunch — Have a delicious lunch at the **Trellis**. Afternoon — She heads to the **Spa of Colonial Williamsburg** for a relaxing massage, manicure, and pedicure. He heads to the **Golden Horseshoe Club** for an afternoon of golf. Wind up your evening together at the **Chef's Kitchen**, where you learn to cook and then dine on a five-course meal with wine.

A FUN WINTER DAY FOR THE FAMILY

Morning — Sit down with the family and enjoy a hearty breakfast at Camp Critter at your resort hotel, **Great Wolf Lodge**. Spend the day playing at the hotel's huge indoor water park, grabbing a quick lunch mid-day. Evening — Head to **Christmas Town** at **Busch Gardens** where kids can visit with Santa and everyone can experience the magic of the holidays.

A FUN SUMMER DAY FOR THE FAMILY

Morning — Get up late and head for the brunch at **Jimmy's Oven & Grill**, then shop at **Yankee Candle** and the **Williamsburg Outlet Mall**. Let the kids design their own bears at the mall's **Camelot Bears**. Lunch — Grab lunch at the **New York Deli**. Afternoon — Spend the rest of the day riding min-race cars, going on rides and playing games at **Go-Karts Plus**.

GIRLS' SHOPPING DAY

Morning — Stop for a quick coffee and pastry at the **Coffee Beanery Café** or your nearest coffee shop, then head to the **Prime Outlets** to shop for new clothes. Lunch — Stop by **Food for Thought** for a bite to eat. Afternoon — Head to the **Williamsburg Pottery** to find a few bargains. Evening — Do some upscale shopping at **Merchant's Square** and wind down with dinner and drinks at the **Blue Talon Bistro**.

COUPLE'S DAY IN YORKTOWN

Morning — Enjoy breakfast at your hotel, the **Duke of York**, then catch some rays on the beach. Afternoon — Grab a late lunch at the **Yorktown Pub**, then go back to the room to shower and take a break. Evening — Get all dressed up and walk over to **Nicks Riverwalk Restaurant** for a romantic dinner followed by a moonlit walk on the beach.

A COLONIAL DAY AND EVENING EXPERIENCE FOR TWO

Morning — Enjoy a hot breakfast buffet at **King's Arm Tavern** while shooting the breeze with Thomas Jefferson or Patrick Henry. Then tour some of the exhibit buildings in **Colonial Williamsburg's Historic Area**. Lunch — Try Welsh Rarebit at **Shields Tavern**. Afternoon — Catch a colonial-style drama at the **Play Booth Theater**, then stroll the gardens of the **Governor's Palace**. Evening — Get dressed up in colonial costumes and head to **Gambols** at **Chowning's Tavern** for an evening of lively colonial entertainment with spirits, music, games, and sing-alongs. Sleep in one of Colonial Williamsburg's quaint colonial houses.

Index

Index

◉ tourist town guides®

Explore America's Fun Places

Books in the *Tourist Town Guides®* series are available at bookstores and online. You can also visit our website for additional book and travel information. The address is:

http://www.touristtown.com

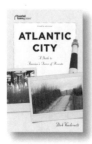

Atlantic City (4th Edition)

This guide will introduce a new facet of Atlantic City that goes beyond the appeal exercised by its lavish casinos. Atlantic City is one of the most popular vacation destinations in the United States.

Price: $14.95; ISBN: 978-1-935455-00-4

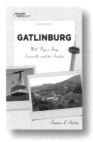

Gatlinburg (2nd Edition)

Whether it is to see the weird and wonderful displays at Ripley's Believe It or Not! Museum, or to get the adrenalin pumping with some outdoor activity or to revel in the extravaganza of Dollywood, people come to the Smokies for a variety of reasons – and they are never disappointed!

Price: $14.95; ISBN: 978-1-935455-04-2

Hilton Head

A barrier island off the coast of South Carolina, Hilton Head is a veritable coastal paradise. This destination guide gives a detailed account of this resort island, tailor made for a coastal vacation.

Price: $14.95; ISBN: 978-1-935455-06-6

Myrtle Beach (2nd Edition)

The sunsets are golden and the pace is relaxed at Myrtle Beach, the beachside playground for vacationers looking for their fill of sun, sand, and surf. Head here for the pristine beaches, the shopping opportunities, the sea of attractions, or simply to kick back and unwind.

Price: $14.95; ISBN: 978-1-935455-01-1

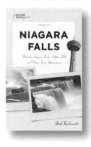

Niagara Falls (3rd Edition)

The spirited descent of the gushing falls may be the lure for you, but in Niagara Falls, it is the smorgasbord of activities and attractions that will keep you coming back for more!

Price: $14.95; ISBN: 978-1-935455-03-5

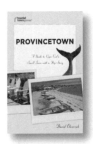

Provincetown

With a rich heritage and proud history, Provincetown is America's oldest art colony, but there is more to this place than its culture. The guide to Provincetown explores its attractions and accommodations, culture and recreation in detail to reveal a vacation destination definitely worth visiting.

Price: $13.95; ISBN: 978-1-935455-07-3

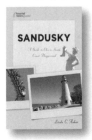

Sandusky

The Cedar Point Amusement Park may be the main reason to visit Sandusky, but this comprehensive guide provides ample reason to stick around and explore Sandusky and the neighboring islands.

Price: $13.95; ISBN: 978-0-9767064-5-8

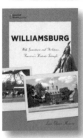

Williamsburg

The lure to explore history is unmistakable in the town, but Williamsburg is so much more than its rich history. Head to this region to discover the modern facets of this quaint town, indulge in activities guaranteed to hook your interest, and step into the past in this historically significant destination.

Price: $14.95; ISBN: 978-1-935455-05-9

Also Available: (See http://www.touristtown.com for details)

Black Hills	Price: $14.95; ISBN: 978-0-9792043-1-9)
Breckenridge	Price: $14.95; ISBN: 978-0-9767064-9-6)
Frankenmuth	Price: $13.95; ISBN: 978-0-9767064-8-9)
Hershey	Price: $13.95; ISBN: 978-0-9792043-8-8)
Jackson Hole	Price: $13.95; ISBN: 978-0-9792043-3-3)
Key West (2nd Edition)	Price: $14.95; ISBN: 978-1-935455-02-8)
Las Vegas	Price: $13.95; ISBN: 978-0-9792043-5-7)
Mackinac	Price: $14.95; ISBN: 978-0-9767064-7-2)
Ocean City	Price: $13.95; ISBN: 978-0-9767064-6-5)
Wisconsin Dells	Price: $13.95; ISBN: 978-0-9792043-9-5)

About the Author

A native Virginian, Lisa Oliver Monroe lives in Richmond with her sons, Mark and Eric. She grew up across the York River from Williamsburg in rural Gloucester County. The water is a main focus of her childhood memories, and she recalls many family boating excursions to isolated York beaches to swim, picnic and search for shells and arrowheads.

Lisa has primarily made her living as a writer. She's worked as a weekly newspaper reporter and photographer, managing editor, technical editor, fact-checker, proofreader, graphic designer and high school teacher. She's published numerous articles on topics ranging from business and healthcare to entertainment and art. Her writing has appeared in regional magazines like *Virginia Living* and *Richmond GRID*. Lisa received a news photography award from the Virginia Press Association, and was recognized by the Richmond chapter of the American Business Women's Association in 2007 for focusing on positive community news as an editor.

Lisa is interested in preserving nature and history, and she firmly believes everyone has a story to tell. In her spare time, she likes to read, write and explore new restaurants, foods, wines and experiences.

www.touristtown.com

ORDER FORM
ON REVERSE SIDE

Tourist Town Guides® is published by:
Channel Lake, Inc.
P.O. Box 1771
New York, NY 10156

ORDER FORM

Telephone: With your credit card handy,
call toll-free 800.592.1566

Fax: Send this form toll-free to 866.794.5507

E-mail: Send the information on this form
to orders@channellake.com

Postal mail: Send this form with payment to Channel Lake, Inc.
P.O. Box 1771, New York, NY, 10156

Your Information: ( ) Do not add me to your mailing list

Name: _____

Address: _____

City: _____ State: _____ Zip: _____

Telephone: _____

E-mail: _____

Book Title(s) / ISBN(s) / Quantity / Price
(see previous page or www.touristtown.com for this information)

_____

_____

_____

Total payment*: $_____

Payment Information: (Circle One)   Visa / Mastercard

Number: _____ Exp: _____

Or, make check payable to: **Channel Lake, Inc.**

** Add the lesser of $6.50 USD or 18% of the total purchase price
for shipping. International orders call or e-mail first! New York
orders add 8% sales tax.*